RO
BIRKDALE

DEDICATED IN MEMORY OF
David Davies
Robert Sommers

Aurum Press
7 Greenland Street, London NW1 0ND

Published 2008 by Aurum Press

Statistics of The 137th Open Championship produced on a
Unisys Computer System

Course map courtesy of Graham Gaches

Assistance with records and research provided by Malcolm Booth,
Peter Lewis, Salvatore Johnson, and www.golfobserver.com

A CIP catalogue record for this book is available
from the British Library

ISBN-13: 978 1 84513 375 7

Designed and produced by Davis Design
Colour retouching by Luciano Retouching Services, Inc.
Printed in Great Britain by Purbrooks

WRITERS
Andy Farrell

Mike Aitken

John Hopkins

Lewine Mair

Alistair Tait

PHOTOGRAPHERS
Getty Images

David Cannon	Tom Reading
Stuart Franklin	Dean Mouhtaropoulos
Scott Halleran	Richard Martin-Roberts
Richard Heathcote	Mark Trowbridge
Ross Kinnaird	*Golf Editors*
Warren Little	
Andy Lyons	Steve Rose
Andrew Redington	*Chief Editor*

EDITOR
Bev Norwood

The Championship Committee

CHAIRMAN
Michael Brown

DEPUTY CHAIRMAN
Rodney James

COMMITTEE

Keith Andrews	Jeremy Monroe
David Bonsall	Richard Souter
Gavin Caldwell	Richard Stocks
George MacGregor	Geoffrey Vero
Jim McArthur	Nigel Watt

ADVISORY MEMBER
Desmond Duffy
Council of National Golf Unions

CHIEF EXECUTIVE
Peter Dawson

DIRECTOR OF CHAMPIONSHIPS
David Hill

DIRECTOR OF RULES AND EQUIPMENT STANDARDS
David Rickman

The R&A is golf's world rules and development body and organiser of The Open Championship. It operates with the consent of more than 130 national and international, amateur and professional organisations, from over 120 countries and on behalf of an estimated 30 million golfers in Europe, Africa, Asia-Pacific and The Americas (outside the USA and Mexico). The United States Golf Association (USGA) is the game's governing body in the United States and Mexico.

Introduction

By Michael Brown

Chairman of the Championship Committee of The R&A

The return to Royal Birkdale for The 137th Open Championship was eagerly anticipated following a number of alterations to the magnificent Birkdale links which once more proved to be a very complete test of the competitors' skills.

The course was in really excellent condition in the run in and attracted universal praise from the players both for its condition and set-up. I must thank Chris Whittle and his team for the tremendous job they did in the lead up and when weather conditions were challenging to say the least.

As last year at Carnoustie, the Championship started in rain at 6.30am on Thursday and that was largely the story of Thursday and Friday with a brisk wind adding to the players' difficulties. The cut came at nine over Birkdale's demanding par at 149. For the weekend the wind got up and we had two days of very windy dry conditions with winds gusting at times to 45mph.

Against this background a thrilling Championship was played out on Sunday with the halfway leader Greg Norman turning the clock back and going all the way head to head with the defending Champion Padraig Harrington, who only finally had some breathing space after the shot of the week at the 17th saw him eagle the hole. Padraig's play on the back nine on Sunday could not be praised highly enough with his shots to the last two holes the stuff of dreams!

I must thank the Royal Birkdale Championship Committee for all their assistance, without which the successful staging of the Championship would not have been possible, all our hundreds of volunteers for their help during the week, and the fans who, once again, attended in huge numbers throughout.

I hope you will find in the following pages an enjoyable reminder of a memorable week of golf.

Michael Brown

Foreword

By Padraig Harrington

A year on and I'm thrilled to be invited to write this Foreword again as it means I am the Champion Golfer of the Year once more.

It was so exciting to become Open Champion in 2007. I have never tired of talking about it but I knew I would not be satisfied with just one major title.

After arriving at Royal Birkdale this year, my first stop was The R&A's Junior Open at Hesketh Golf Club where I showed the Claret Jug to more than 100 competitors from some 70 countries, some of which I'm sure will develop into champions of the future.

Unfortunately, I arrived carrying a wrist injury that played havoc with my preparations. I only managed to play nine holes in practice but in retrospect it kept me fresh ahead of the four gruelling rounds to come. Royal Birkdale was in great condition, very fairly set up and together with the tough weather conditions provided an excellent stage for The 137th Open Championship. Aside from significantly less time on the range and the course, I kept everything else the same as the previous year. My family, Bob Rotella and Bob Torrance were all on hand to provide support and by Wednesday night I was ready to play through any pain to defend my title.

In the end I think my wrist injury provided a welcome distraction to the pressures of being defending Champion. From the early Thursday morning start, in some of the toughest conditions I have ever played in, to partnering Greg Norman in the final group on Sunday afternoon, my mind stayed focused on one shot at a time. Last year, winning for the first time was obviously very special. This year, managing to produce my very best golf on the back nine of the final round to win by four shots, was even more satisfying and certainly relatively less stressful.

I have loved my year as Open Champion and I am thrilled that I get the chance to do it again. I can only hope that being this year's Champion Golfer of the Year lives up to last year.

The Venue

A Truly Special Course

By Andy Farrell

The Open Championship returns to Royal Birkdale for the ninth time on the Lancashire course.

It is often referred to as the best course in England. And, if you want to bring the rest of Britain into the discussion, only Muirfield can be mentioned.

Few would argue with that assertion. Royal Birkdale routinely features towards the top of the leaderboard when polls of the best courses in the British Isles are conducted. The same view can be found when canvassing amateur club players or the leading professionals. Truly, it must be something special.

It helps that it is located somewhere special: on the 4,000 year-old Sefton dune system that is home to such diverse wildlife, particularly sand lizards, natterjack toads, and skylarks, as well as rare flora and fauna. Birkdale Hills, offering majestic panoramic views of the Lancashire coastline and out to the choppy waters of the Irish Sea, is the area home to soaring dunes just south of Southport and west of

The green at No 13 (left) is beautifully located in front of tall sandhills. The Art Deco clubhouse (preceding pages) looks almost like a ship.

Birkdale Village. It was here in 1897 the members of the then Birkdale Golf Club moved after eight years playing on their original nine-hole layout.

But while God provided such a natural playground for the stick and ball game, the course has been refined by man many times over the years. If inland courses are more obviously manufactured, and links courses tend to evolve, throughout its history Birkdale has been sculpted into the finest Championship challenge of its day.

This process really started in 1935, when Fred Hawtree and J H Taylor, the five-time Open Champion, redesigned the layout. At the same time a new clubhouse was built, reminiscent of a ship sailing among the dunes, in the Art Deco style. The club had to wait until 1954 to stage its first Open Championship, by which time royal patronage had been granted. But after a second Open in 1961, further alterations had to be made by Frank Hawtree, son of Fred, to accommodate the huge crowds that had followed Arnold Palmer to victory. The changes included the introduction of a new par-3 at the 12th hole (replacing the old short 17th), which remains one of the finest holes on the course.

The No 2 green is well bunkered in front.

So it will come as no surprise that for its ninth Open — only the Old Course at St Andrews has hosted the Championship more often since 1954 — more changes were made, with Martin Hawtree becoming the third generation of his family to work on the links. Changes were made to 16 of the 18 holes, with only the 12th and another short hole, the seventh, remaining unscathed. With The Open not having been played here for 10 years, during which time the game has changed so much, once again the course underwent a makeover. Six new tees added 155 yards to the course, making it still a modest 7,173 by today's standards, but most of the alterations were designed to make the players think about every shot. Bunkers were moved, redesigned, 20 new ones were added, 14 removed. New undulations were added to the surrounds of several greens, while the 17th green was moved back and completed redesigned. Such were the contours on the putting surface at the par-5 that this was perhaps the most discussed of the changes.

But of the need to update the links, Peter Dawson, the chief executive of The R&A, was in no doubt. "Royal Birkdale has always been regarded by the players as a great venue," he said. "It's very popular with the players. They think it's a terrific course. What you see is what you get; it's very fair. But things move on, and we decided in combination with the Royal Birkdale Club, and with our architect Martin Hawtree, that some changes were necessary to meet the challenge of the modern-day player. We are very pleased with the outcome."

Perhaps, most importantly, the course's main characteristics were retained. Peter Thomson, who won his first Open at Birkdale in 1954 and his fifth in 1965, called it a "man-sized course but not a monster." The Australian added: "If there is just one tiny part of your game that is not quite right, the great course will find it out, no matter how hard you try to hide it." Under this definition, Birkdale passes the test of greatest.

A similarity with Muirfield is that the course loops back to the clubhouse, rather than being an out-and-back links like many on the Open rota. "Its strongest asset is the variety of the direction in which the holes play," said Tom Watson, yet another five-time winner of The Open and the 1983 Champion at Birkdale. "There's a multitude of directions, so that the wind changes all the time from hole to hole, from all different angles — downwind, headwinds, crosswinds."

Another feature of the Hawtree-Taylor layout is that the holes run between the dunes, rather than over them as at other links. It means the fairways are generally flat, other than for subtle undulations, with an absence of blind shots. Perhaps it is this factor that makes the course so welcoming for players who have not grown up playing links golf.

For no particular style is best suited to the course. Thomson was a thinker who plotted his way around a course, taking hazards out of play with wonderfully controlled golf. His victory in 1965 he considered his finest, as by now the field for The Open included all the best Americans, led by Palmer, Jack Nicklaus, and defending Champion Tony Lema.

Yet could there be a greater contrast with Palmer, the winner four years earlier, whose aggressive style helped popularise the game so much? He thrashed the ball mighty distances and, facing a gale in the second round, took it on in red-blooded fashion with five birdies in the first six holes. Later in the Championship he called a one-stroke penalty on himself because, unseen by anyone else, his ball had moved in a bunker. Then there came the shot of legend, his six-iron blast from a bush at the then 15th (now the 16th hole, where a plaque commemorates the outrageous stroke) which put him back

Trouble awaits at No 7 with a bunker short and left of the green.

No 14 is a strong par-3 hole played from an elevated tee.

on the green and on the way to the first of two Open victories. It also consolidated his reputation as the player every other golfer wanted to be.

Lee Trevino arrived in 1971 as the winner of the US Open and the Canadian Open. He went on to a remarkable hat-trick, but only after taking 7 at the 17th hole after his drive had finished in a horrid lie on top of a sandhill. He survived to win by one stroke from Lu Liang Huan, from Taiwan, or "Mr Lu" as he had become known during the week.

Americans really have enjoyed great success here. In 1976 it was Johnny Miller who took the title during his brief but exalted spell as the best player in the world. Watson claimed his fifth Open title in 1983 with a superb two iron to within 20 feet of the hole at the 18th. Then in 1998 Mark O'Meara triumphed in a playoff over Brian Watts, an American who had played with success in Japan. It was a remarkable year for O'Meara, who had won the Masters three months earlier for his first major victory — all this resulting during the time he was mentoring the young Tiger Woods when he first came on the scene.

In between Watson and O'Meara came an Australian, Ian Baker-Finch in 1991. Baker-Finch produced some sumptuous scoring, with 64 in the third round and then going to the turn on the final day in 29 strokes with birdies at five of the first seven holes. Twice before he had been in the final pairing on a Sunday at The Open, both times at St Andrews, and not managed to challenge. This was his time, a triumph put into stark contrast by his subsequent loss of form.

So eight Opens and no home or European winners? Not even in the Ryder Cup, twice staged at Birkdale in 1965 and 1969. There was drama aplenty, however, on the second of those occasions, with the finale coming when Nicklaus conceded Tony Jacklin's putt on the final green to ensure the match was tied. Nicklaus said: "I didn't think you were going to miss it. But I wasn't going to give you the chance." America still retained the cup.

Their dominance in the transatlantic competition was to come to an end, however, with the emergence of Severiano Ballesteros and other leading players from Europe. It was at Birkdale in 1976 that a 19

Round Royal Birkdale

No 1 • 450 yards Par 4
A tough opening hole, slight dogleg right-to-left, that requires a well-placed drive in order to set up for a demanding second shot. The bunkering has been tightened into the green and new greenside mounding and contouring adds to the difficulty of the approach.

No 2 • 421 yards Par 4
Another slight dogleg to the left, this time into the prevailing wind. The tee shot has been toughened by the addition of 45 yards of new mounding on the left of the fairway and two new bunkers on the right, both features at the driving distance. The green is well bunkered at the front.

No 3 • 451 yards Par 4
A new tee set back in the high dunes means a very challenging tee shot with new bunkering to the left side of the fairway at drive distance. A previously flat green surround is transformed with new mounding and contouring and the addition of a bunker, front right, putting a premium on approach shot accuracy.

No 4 • 201 yards Par 3
A very challenging par-3 with tightened bunkering into the green and new mounding introduced to the right of the green. Three bunkers guard the front and left of the green, while another awaits on the right.

No 5 • 346 yards Par 4
A short par-4 doglegging to the right. Tightened bunkering into the green demands accuracy from the second shot, and a greater variety of hole locations is made possible by widening the right side of the green. Still it is a narrow right, sloping back to front.

No 6 • 499 yards Par 4
A magnificent par-4, a dogleg to the right around a high-faced bunker and high mounds. A new back tee challenges the opening shot and new bunkering features on the left side of the fairway, at 303 yards, and also set into the left side of the green, which angles away from right to left.

No 7 • 178 yards Par 3
No modifications were required to this outstanding par-3, played to an upturned saucer of a green surrounded by seven deep pot bunkers. Any escape will need a delicate touch.

No 8 • 457 yards Par 4
The challenge of the tee shot is increased dramatically by added fairway bunkering, left at 267 yards and right at 307 yards. The hole is a dogleg to the left with the green protected by bunkers at its entrance and extended to provide greater variety of pin positions.

No 9 • 414 yards Par 4
The fairway has been moved left to produce a left-to-right dogleg. New mounding on the right adds danger for those tempted to cut the corner. A new front left bunker presents another hazard for the second shot, matching the one on the right, while trouble awaits over the green.

No 10 • 408 yards Par 4
A relatively short par-4, but a sweeping dogleg to the left. Strategic bunkering has been repositioned on the left side of the fairway. Anyone hitting a weak tee shot will find this hole extremely demanding.

No 11 • 436 yards Par 4
Into the prevailing westerly wind this is a tough par-4 from the new back tee. The green, angled to the right, offers many potentially demanding pin positions. Club selection here will be vital.

No 12 • 184 yards Par 3
A superb par-3, which has not been modified in any way. A controlled fade is required into the prevailing wind, which comes from the right. Deep bunkers and banks of rough protect the small green.

No 13 • 499 yards Par 4
A tough par-4 made more so by new fairway bunkers on both left and right. Great views from the elevated tee, but the drive needs to be long and accurate, followed by a strong second shot into a green beautifully located in front of tall sandhills.

No 14 • 201 yards Par 3
Already a strong par-3 but enhanced by more aggressive bunkering and contouring around the green. Played from an elevated tee which is protected from the prevailing wind. Danger lurks all around the putting surface.

No 15 • 544 yards Par 5
The addition of new fairway bunkering and mounding at the green approach makes this a demanding par-5 which is difficult to attack. In all, 15 bunkers line the narrow fairway. The removal of trees on the left opens up the links aspect of the hole.

No 16 • 439 yards Par 4
A new back tee has made this a fearsome tee shot against the prevailing westerly wind. Re-contouring around the green and the removal of trees to the rear present an open appearance and a less defined target. The approach shot is to an elevated green which is well protected by deep bunkers.

No 17 • 572 yards Par 5
The drive needs to be threaded between two huge sand dunes, avoiding two new bunkers on the right side of the fairway at 316 and 320 yards. A more demanding second shot was created by the ingress of bunkers and mounds, narrowing the fairway. The green has been moved back and raised, and is severely contoured.

No 18 • 473 yards Par 4
Remains a strong finishing hole for an Open Championship. New fairway bunkering has been added at 304 yards, on the left side of the fairway, challenging the tee shot, which already is threatened by out of bounds on the right. Three bunkers, two left, one right, guard the entrance to the green.

The approach shot at No 16 is to an elevated green, well protected by deep bunkers.

A plaque notes the location of Arnold Palmer's famous shot in 1961 at No 15, which is now No 16.

year-old Spaniard with broken English first displayed his incredible talents to the world. Ballesteros gave Miller a run for his money, but the American was too strong with a closing 66. But at the final hole it was the Spaniard who stole the show with an exquisitely judged chip-and-run between two bunkers and onto the green.

Of course, a brilliant short game was to be the hallmark of the Spaniard's career, but in 1998 the 18th hole saw an even more dramatic moment — and possibly the loudest cheer ever heard on an Open links. Justin Rose was an amateur still days away from his 18th birthday, but there he was, the darling of the home gallery, contending for the title. He could not quite reach the playoff between O'Meara and Watts, but at the 18th, from 30 yards short of the green, he pitched over a bunker and into the hole.

After a difficult period after he first turned professional — which happened the next day — Rose returned in 2008 as one of the best players in the world. But Woods, who finished only a stroke behind O'Meara and Watts in 1998, did not. Following his dramatic victory in the US Open, after a 19-hole playoff against Rocco Mediate and with a damaged knee and stress fractures of his tibia, the former Open Champion was forced to undergo surgery for the second time in two months and miss the rest of the season. He would be missed, but surely now the Championship was wide open. Yet it is never a question of who must be overcome but what, and, at Birkdale, that is always a mighty challenge.

Exempt Competitors

Name, Country	Category	Name, Country	Category
Robert Allenby, Australia	7	Brendan Jones, Australia	25
Stephen Ames, Canada	7, 14	Shintaro Kai, Japan	27
Stuart Appleby, Australia	7, 19	Robert Karlsson, Sweden	7
Woody Austin, USA	7, 15, 19	Martin Kaymer, Germany	7
Aaron Baddeley, Australia	7, 15	Jerry Kelly**, USA	7
Bart Bryant, USA	16	Simon Khan, England	10
Angel Cabrera, Argentina	5, 7, 11, 19	Anthony Kim, USA	7
Mark Calcavecchia, USA	3, 15	James Kingston, South Africa	22
Michael Campbell, New Zealand	11	Soren Kjeldsen, Denmark	5
Paul Casey, England	5, 7	Pablo Larrazabal, Spain	9
KJ Choi, Korea	1, 7, 15, 19	Paul Lawrie, Scotland	3, 4
Stewart Cink, USA	1, 7, 19	Tom Lehman, USA	3
Tim Clark, South Africa	7	Justin Leonard, USA	3, 7
Ben Curtis, USA	1, 3, 4	Wen Chong Liang, China	20
John Daly, USA	3	Sandy Lyle, Scotland	3
Nick Dougherty, England	5	Hunter Mahan, USA	1, 7, 15, 19
David Duval, USA	3, 4	Prayad Marksaeng, Thailand	26
Ernie Els, South Africa	1, 3, 4, 5, 7, 15, 19	Michio Matsumura, Japan	26
Niclas Fasth, Sweden	5, 7	Graeme McDowell, Northern Ireland	8
Richard Finch, England	8	Damien McGrane, Republic of Ireland	8
David Frost, South Africa	10	Rocco Mediate, USA	17
Jim Furyk, USA	7, 15, 19, 23	Phil Mickelson, USA	7, 12, 13, 14, 15, 19
Sergio Garcia, Spain	1, 5, 7, 14, 15	Colin Montgomerie, Scotland	5
Lucas Glover, USA	19	Greg Norman, Australia	3
Retief Goosen, South Africa	5, 7, 11, 19	Geoff Ogilvy, Australia	7, 11, 15, 19
Richard Green, Australia	1	Sean O'Hair, USA	7
Todd Hamilton, USA	3, 4	Nick O'Hern, Australia	19
Anders Hansen, Denmark	5, 6	Mark O'Meara, USA	3, 4
Soren Hansen, Denmark	5, 7	Rod Pampling, Australia	7
Peter Hanson, Sweden	5	Craig Parry, Australia	21
Padraig Harrington, Republic of Ireland	1, 3, 4, 5, 7	Pat Perez**, USA	7
Gregory Havret, France	5	Ian Poulter, England	7
Benjamin Hebert*, France	31	Jeff Quinney, USA	7
J B Holmes, USA	7	Andres Romero, Argentina	1, 5, 7
Charles Howell III, USA	15, 19	Justin Rose, England	5, 7, 15
David Howell, England	6	Rory Sabbatini, South Africa	7, 15, 19
Ryuji Imada, Japan	16	Reinier Saxton*, Netherlands	29
Trevor Immelman, South Africa	7, 12, 19	Adam Scott, Australia	7, 15, 19
Hiroshi Iwata, Japan	27	Vijay Singh, Fiji	7, 13, 15, 19
Fredrik Jacobson, Sweden	18	Heath Slocum**, USA	7
Miguel Angel Jimenez, Spain	6, 7	David Smail, New Zealand	21
Zach Johnson, USA	7, 12, 15, 19	Brandt Snedeker, USA	7, 15

Name, Country	Category	Name, Country	Category
Henrik Stenson, Sweden	5, 7	Camilo Villegas**, Colombia	7
Richard Sterne, South Africa	5, 7	Tom Watson, USA	3, 28
Graeme Storm, England	5	Boo Weekley, USA	7
Scott Strange, Australia	9	Mike Weir, Canada	1, 7, 19
Steve Stricker, USA	1, 7, 15, 19	Lee Westwood, England	5, 7
Hideto Tanihara, Japan	25	Jay Williamson, USA	18
Yoshinobu Tsukada, Japan	26	Oliver Wilson, England	7
Scott Verplank, USA	7, 15, 19	Azuma Yano, Japan	26

* Denotes amateurs   **Denotes reserves

Key to Exemptions from Regional, Local Final and International Final Qualifying

Exemptions for 2008 were granted to the following:

(1) First 10 and anyone tying for 10th place in the 2007 Open Championship at Carnoustie.

(2) Past Open Champions born between 20 July 1942 - 19 July 1948.

(3) Past Open Champions aged 60 or under on 20 July 2008.

(4) The Open Champions for 1998-2007.

(5) First 20 in the PGA European Tour Final Order of Merit for 2007.

(6) The BMW PGA Championship winners for 2006-2008.

(7) The first 50 players on the Official World Golf Ranking for Week 21, 2008.

(8) First 3 and anyone tying for 3rd place, not exempt having applied (7) above, in the top 20 of the PGA European Tour Order of Merit for 2008 on completion of the 2008 BMW PGA Championship.

(9) First 2 European Tour members and any European Tour members tying for 2nd place, not exempt, in a cumulative money list taken from all official PGA European Tour events from the Official World Golf Ranking for Week 19 up to and including the Open de France ALSTOM and including The US Open.

(10) The leading player, not exempt having applied (9) above, in the first 5 and ties of each of the 2008 European Open and the 2008 Barclays Scottish Open. Ties will be decided by the better final round score and, if still tied, by the better third round score and then by the better second round score. If still tied, a hole by hole card playoff will take place starting at the 18th hole of the final round.

(11) The US Open Champions for 2004-2008.

(12) The US Masters Champions for 2004-2008.

(13) The USPGA Champions for 2003-2007.

(14) The USPGA Tour Players Champions for 2006-2008.

(15) First 20 on the Official Money List of the USPGA Tour for 2007.

(16) First 3 and anyone tying for 3rd place, not exempt having applied (7) above, in the top 20 of the Official Money List of the USPGA Tour for 2008 on completion of the Crowne Plaza Invitational at Colonial.

(17) First 2 USPGA Tour members and any USPGA Tour members tying for 2nd place, not exempt, in a cumulative money list taken from the USPGA Tour Players Championship and the five USPGA Tour events leading up to and including the 2008 AT&T National.

(18) The leading player, not exempt having applied (17) above, in the first 5 and ties of each of the 2008 AT&T National and the 2008 John Deere Classic. Ties will be decided by the better final round score and, if still tied, by the better third round score and then by the better second round score. If still tied, a hole by hole card playoff will take place starting at the 18th hole of the final round.

(19) Playing members of the 2007 Presidents Cup teams.

(20) First and anyone tying for 1st place on the Order of Merit of the Asian Tour for 2007.

(21) First 2 and anyone tying for 2nd place on the Order of Merit of the Tour of Australasia for 2007.

(22) First and anyone tying for 1st place on the Order of Merit of the Southern Africa PGA Sunshine Tour for 2007.

(23) The Canadian Open Champion for 2007.

(24) The Japan Open Champion for 2007.

(25) First 2 and anyone tying for 2nd place, not exempt, on the Official Money List of the Japan Golf Tour for 2007.

(26) The leading 4 players, not exempt, in the 2008 Mizuno Open Yomiuri Classic. Ties will be decided by the better final round score and, if still tied, by the better third round score and then by the better second round score. If still tied, a hole by hole card playoff will take place starting at the 18th hole of the final round.

(27) First 2 and anyone tying for 2nd place, not exempt having applied (26) above, in a cumulative money list taken from all official Japan Golf Tour events from the 2008 Japan PGA Championship up to and including the 2008 Mizuno Open Yomiuri Classic.

(28) The Senior Open Champion for 2007.

(29) The Amateur Champion for 2008.

(30) The US Amateur Champion for 2007.

(31) The European Individual Amateur Champion for 2007. *(29) to (31) are only applicable if the entrant concerned is still an amateur on 17 July 2008.*

Local Final Qualifying
7-8 July

Hillside
Jamie Elson, England	67	73	140
Chris Wood*, England	71	72	143
Rohan Blizard*, Australia	71	72	143
Jean Van de Velde, France	70	73	143

Southport & Ainsdale
Thomas Sherreard*, England	72	69	141
Jon Bevan, England	70	71	141
Jamie Howarth[P], England	70	73	143
Gary Boyd[P], England	71	72	143

West Lancashire
Philip Walton, Rep. of Ireland	72	70	142
Barry Hume, Scotland	70	75	145
Jonathan Lomas[P], England	75	72	147
Peter Appleyard[P], England	72	75	147

1 Hillside
2 Southport & Ainsdale
3 West Lancashire

ROYAL BIRKDALE

LIVERPOOL

* Denotes amateurs   [P] Qualified after playoff

The Starting Field

"G. In the event of an exempt player withdrawing from the Championship or further places becoming available in the starting field after IFQ Europe and IFQ America, these places will be allocated in ranking order of entrants from the Official World Golf Ranking at the time that intimation of the withdrawal is received by the Championship Committee. Any withdrawals following the issue of OWGR Week 27 will be taken in ranking order from OWGR Week 27."

Camilo Villegas, Colombia, replaced Tiger Woods
Pat Perez, USA, replaced David Toms

Heath Slocum, USA, replaced Toru Taniguchi
Jerry Kelly, USA, replaced Luke Donald

Jean Van de Velde

Jamie Howarth

Barry Hume

Thomas Sherreard

International Final Qualifying

ASIA   25-26 March

Sentosa   *Singapore*

Danny Chia, Malaysia	69	69	138
Adam Blyth, Australia	73	66	139
Chih-Bing Lam[(P)], Singapore	72	68	140
Angelo Que[(P)], Philippines	69	71	140

Danny Chia

AMERICA   30 June

Dearborn Country Club   *Dearborn, Michigan*

Paul Goydos, USA	65	66	131
Michael, Letzig, USA	67	66	133
Doug LaBelle II, USA	68	66	134
Rich Beem[(P)], USA	67	68	135
Craig Barlow[(P)], USA	66	69	135
Kevin Stadler[(P)], USA	69	66	135
Davis Love III[(P)], USA	67	68	135

TPC Michigan   *Dearborn, Michigan*

Jeff Overton, USA	63	67	130
John Rollins, USA	67	69	136
Tim Petrovic, USA	67	70	137
Matt Kuchar, USA	69	68	137
Alex Cejka, Germany	68	69	137
Scott McCarron USA	71	67	138
Thomas Gillis [(P)], USA	71	68	139

Paul Goydos

AUSTRALASIA   5 February

The Lakes   *Sydney, Australia*

Andrew Tampion, Australia	67	71	138
Bradley Lamb, Australia	71	70	141
Ewan Porter, Australia	72	69	141
Peter Fowler, Australia	71	70	141

Andrew Tampion

EUROPE 30 June

Sunningdale *Berkshire, England*

Simon Wakefield, England	65	68	133
Ariel Canete, Argentina	67	66	133
Johan Edfors, Sweden	67	67	134
Jean-Baptiste Gonnet, France	66	68	134
Ross Fisher, England	66	68	134
Gregory Bourdy, France	66	68	134
Paul Waring, England	68	67	135
Thomas Aiken, South Africa	68	67	135
Alexander Noren, Sweden	72	63	135
Pelle Edberg, Sweden	68	67	135
Anthony Wall, England	66	69	135
Jose-Filipe Lima, Portugal	66	69	135
David Horsey, England	68	67	135
Martin Wiegele, Austria	69	66	135
Phillip Archer, England	67	68	135
Steve Webster, England	68	67	135
Peter Baker[P], England	70	66	136
Simon Dyson[P], England	65	71	136

Simon Wakefield

AFRICA 15-16 January

Royal Johannesburg *Johannesburg,*
& Kensington *South Africa*

Joshua Cunliffe, South Africa	65	65	130
Darren Fichardt, South Africa	68	63	131
Douglas McGuigan, Scotland	67	67	134
Hennie Otto, South Africa	69	65	134

Joshua Cunliffe

Royal Birkdale

Welcome To The Brutal Open

By Andy Farrell

Conditions get rough at Royal Birkdale as only McDowell, Mediate, and Allenby finish under par.

Who needs *You Know Who* anyway? Not when you have Rocco Mediate. The 45 year-old American was the runner-up at the US Open and earned a special place in the hearts of all golf fans for the way he pushed Tiger Woods to the very limit before the world No 1 claimed a victory of scarcely credible proportions at the 91st hole. That was on the cliffs of Torrey Pines in the Californian sunshine a month earlier.

Apart from being by the sea, Royal Birkdale on the opening day of The 137th Open Championship had little in common. It was wet. It was cold. It was very windy. Summer it was not. But just when it appeared no one would finish under par for the day, along came Mediate and his endearingly sunny disposition to birdie the last two holes and claim a place at the top of the leaderboard with 69. It was a trick repeated by both Graeme McDowell and

---

Graeme McDowell's 69 included only one bogey on his card.

Robert Allenby for a three-way tie at the top.

McDowell, just crowned the Barclays Scottish Open champion at Loch Lomond the previous Sunday, had been the sole first-round leader at Hoylake two years ago. The Northern Irishman learnt his golf at Portrush and never was that experience more valuable than on a day like this. Mediate could not say the same. "I have no explanation whatsoever," he admitted of his status on the leaderboard. "No idea why that happened."

Perhaps, after staring Tiger in the eyes, nothing felt quite so intimidating. "It's been a great ride, it's been a lot of fun," Mediate said. "I think it has done nothing but make me a better player, even though I did not win the golf tournament. Some people forget that. I'd like a chance to be in contention again and see if I can handle it all again and maybe do one better.

"I'd rather Tiger be here than not," Mediate added. "But does it take anything away from this week? Absolutely not. This is one of the greatest tournaments ever. I think it's going to be just as nerve-wracking, just as exciting. It's all about what's in here," he said pointing at his chest.

'Bloody miserable' (weather) declared Craig Parry, the Australian veteran who was first off in the Championship.

Thursday Weather

Early in day, cloudy with rain heavy at times, light rain and mainly dry in afternoon and evening. Winds SW at 20mph, gusts to 25-30mph.

In recovering from a number of back injuries, Mediate had shown plenty of internal fortitude. Even early in this most demanding of Opens, it was obvious such qualities would come to the fore. "It's all about whoever handles the insanity best," Mediate said. "There was definitely dread this morning seeing the weather conditions. But once you get inside the ropes and off the first tee, it's like, let's see what we've got today. There's so many ways to get it done around here. The golf courses were built so beautifully back then. It allows you to play in these conditions because that's what they built it for."

All week the wind was blowing in from the west off the Irish Sea. Overnight on Wednesday came the rain, and for the morning starters it was a gruesome spectacle. Welcome to the brutal Open. Craig Parry, the Australian born in Sunshine, Victoria,

First Round Leaders

HOLE	1	2	3	4	5	6	7	8	9	10	11	12	13	14	15	16	17	18	
PAR	4	4	4	3	4	4	3	4	4	4	4	3	4	3	5	4	5	4	TOTAL
Rocco Mediate	5	4	5	3	5	4	3	3	4	4	4	3	3	3	5	4	4	3	69
Graeme McDowell	4	4	4	3	4	5	3	4	4	4	4	3	4	3	5	4	4	3	69
Robert Allenby	5	4	4	3	4	5	4	4	4	3	4	2	4	3	5	4	4	3	69
Greg Norman	5	4	3	3	4	4	3	4	4	4	4	3	5	3	5	4	4	4	70
Adam Scott	4	4	4	3	4	3	3	4	4	4	4	3	4	3	4	5	6	4	70
Bart Bryant	4	4	4	3	4	5	3	4	4	4	3	3	4	3	6	4	5	3	70
Retief Goosen	4	4	4	3	6	4	3	4	3	4	4	2	4	2	6	5	4	5	71
Mike Weir	5	4	4	3	3	6	3	4	4	4	4	3	3	3	5	6	3	4	71
Jim Furyk	5	5	4	3	5	4	3	4	4	4	4	3	4	2	5	4	4	4	71
Gregory Havret	4	4	4	4	4	4	4	4	4	4	5	3	4	3	4	5	3	4	71
Fredrik Jacobson	6	4	4	3	4	5	2	4	4	4	4	3	3	3	5	4	4	5	71
Peter Hanson	4	3	4	3	4	5	3	3	4	5	5	4	4	2	5	4	5	4	71
Simon Wakefield	4	5	5	3	5	4	3	4	3	4	4	3	4	3	5	4	4	4	71
Anthony Wall	3	4	4	4	4	5	3	4	4	3	5	4	4	3	4	4	5	4	71

hit the opening tee shot at 6.30am and returned 77. "Bloody miserable," was his succinct verdict. "It was an honour to hit the first tee shot, but after that it got really hard. I was home a couple of weeks ago and we were swimming in the ocean in the middle of winter. It was brutal out there today."

Other early starters, like Simon Dyson and Jerry Kelly, neither of whom broke 80, felt the tees at the 11th and the 16th holes should have been moved up. But generally the course set-up was praised, Peter Dawson, the chief executive of The R&A, revealing at the end of the week that he had had fewer players pounding on his door to complain than at any recent Open.

"I think this is the best Open I've ever played in," said Greg Norman. "I think the golf course has been set up by The R&A about the fairest and toughest I've ever seen. It doesn't favour one particular player or style of player. It's very well balanced and gives an opportunity to everyone to put a number on the board." What was Norman doing here? How did he score 70? All would be revealed later.

Sandy Lyle, struggling with injured fingers which

Rocco Mediate continued his inspired play at Royal Birkdale.

Excerpts FROM THE Press

"There could not be a greater contrast between the burnished fairways at Hoylake two years ago and the saturated dunes here at Birkdale, yet the story remains the same. Ulsterman Graeme McDowell, just as he was in 2006, is the first-round leader of The Open Championship."

—Derek Lawrenson, *Daily Mail*

"Ben Curtis, who confounded the world of golf by winning The Open at Royal St George's in 2003, drove his opening tee shot here not onto the fairway but towards car park C. He was so far out of bounds he could have picked up a parking ticket."

—Tim Glover, *The Independent*

"The British challenge for The 137th Open at Birkdale was alive and kicking yesterday. Those who started the day with high hopes ended it, for the most part, with them still intact, assuming no one went down with pneumonia overnight."

—Claire Middleton, *The Daily Telegraph*

"The last time Justin Rose played Royal Birkdale in earnest, as a teen-age amateur, he said he felt like Jack Nicklaus, such was the tumultuous response of the gallery as he stepped onto every tee and approached every green. Yesterday, 10 years on, he must have felt more like Jacques Cousteau."

—Alan Fraser, *Daily Mail*

Robert Allenby, here on No 12, knew he would eventually hole the putts.

went numb, retired after playing 10 holes in 11 over par, while Rich Beem, also injured, withdrew after reaching the turn in 12 over. Vijay Singh had 80, as did his playing partners Hunter Mahan and Reinier Saxton, the Amateur champion from the Netherlands. "It was miserable, miserable, miserable," Singh said. Ernie Els also had 80, his worst score ever in an Open, despite being one of the few morning starters not to drop a shot over the first five holes. His round unravelled with three 6s in a row from the 14th for a triple bogey, a bogey, and a double bogey.

Birkdale's start is not easy at the best of times, and these were the worst of times. The first two fairways were the hardest to hit

Robert Allenby
An Aussie's Local Knowledge

This Open Championship began for Robert Allenby with a little more local knowledge of the Royal Birkdale links than most. No wonder he managed to compile a one-under-par 69 to share the first-day lead with Rocco Mediate and Graeme McDowell.

The 37 year-old was contending in his third Open on the Southport course. Allenby not only had that experience to draw on, but the knowledge of a former Champion.

Allenby teed it up in the 1991 Open Championship as a wide-eyed and bushy-tailed 20 year-old amateur eager to learn about the oldest form of golf. He missed the cut. However, what he gained more than made up for his disappointment. He was able to pick the Champion's brain.

"I was very fortunate to qualify as an amateur back in 1991, and Ian Baker-Finch was very kind to allow me to play two practice rounds with him," Allenby said.

Armed with that knowledge, Allenby secured a top-20 finish, joint 19th place, in 1998. Needless to say, he wanted to do better when he turned up for The 137th Open. He did the natural thing: He sought out Baker-Finch in his last practice round.

"I really wanted to know the golf course. I wanted to know where everything was," Allenby said. "I think my preparation this week was probably better than any other year I've ever been here. I got a lot of knowledge from Finchy about his win. We had a little chat about the golf course and the way it was playing."

The advice Baker-Finch gave his younger compatriot paid off, especially on the inward nine. Allenby bogeyed the first, sixth, and seventh holes to go to the turn in 37, but he hauled those shots back and more with the way he attacked the last nine.

Five iron was his weapon of choice in taming Royal Birkdale in the brutal conditions of the opening round. He hit that club to 15 feet on the 10th and holed the birdie putt. He manoeuvred his five-iron shot into the wind at the 184-yard, par-3 12th hole to 10 feet and drained that putt too.

Allenby favoured a four iron for his second shot at the 572-yard, par-5 17th and watched as his ball ended up 10 feet from the hole. The eagle putt narrowly missed but gave the Australian another birdie. A fourth followed at the 18th when he hit sand wedge to 20 feet.

"I hit a lot of good shots. I just didn't make a lot of putts on the first nine," Allenby said. "But I knew that if I kept hitting the ball well there were definitely some opportunities to make some birdies."

With four PGA Tour victories, four European Tour wins, and 12 Australasian Tour titles, no one was surprised to see the gritty Australian atop the leaderboard.

Least of all Ian Baker-Finch.

—Alistair Tait

---

with the gale across from the left at the first and directly into at the second. The first two holes were among the top three hardest for the day, while the sixth, where only 10 percent of the field reached the green in the regulation two strokes, was inevitably the hardest of all. On days like this it played more like the par-5 it once was.

Phil Mickelson hooked his second shot on the sixth up onto the dunes on the right, but unlike Mark O'Meara in the third round in 1998, his ball was not found. He had to drop back where his tee shot finished and took a triple-bogey 7 on the way to 79. Lee Westwood made an adventurous 5. On the bank of a bunker for two, in sand for three, he had a 20-foot putt for a bogey until, after marking, lifting, and replacing the ball on the green, it rolled off the front edge. Then he chipped in.

After a poor start in which Westwood bogeyed

Out in 40, Lee Westwood came home in 35.

At No 6, Justin Rose 'did well to make double bogey.'

Keeping dry was a struggle, as KJ Choi demonstrated.

the first and the third holes and took a double bogey at the second, it was an escape that settled the Englishman who was so full of confidence after his third-place finish at the US Open. Out in 40, he came home in 35. If he needed any inspiration to keep battling, it came from Ben Curtis. The 2003 Open Champion hit his first tee shot out of bounds and opened with 7 and then scored 6 on the second. A 78 followed, but the American would work his way up the leaderboard over the next few days.

It was the sort of day when even a bogey at the first got a player's name on the leaderboard. For much of the morning par led the way. Tom Watson birdied the first from three feet but dropped a shot at the next. The five-time Champion was the first of 16 players to stand under par during the day. KJ Choi was the next, but he also only lasted one hole. Japan's Shintaro Kai birdied the first and parred the next two before a 4 at the short fourth. Robert Karlsson picked up an opening 3 and then did not drop a shot until the sixth.

Watson, at 58 the oldest man in the field, was enjoying the battle with the elements. Birkdale's

After his 70, Adam Scott felt his round was 'wasted' by bogeys at Nos 16 and 17.

1983 Champion told his playing companion, Justin Rose, that the day reminded him of the opening round at Muirfield in 1980 when he and Lee Trevino scored 68s and "lapped the field." Both Watson and Rose had 74s, the 27 year-old Englishman on his return to the scene of his amazing performance as an amateur 10 years earlier. Ironically, now Europe's No 1 as the Order of Merit winner in 2007, this time Rose would not contend for the Claret Jug, but he could see why Watson had won five of them. "He is awesome," Rose said. "There's a lot I can take from his game. How he strikes the ball is incredible, the flight of his ball, and the way he reads the greens. I love the way he putts, with a rappy sort of stroke, which I think is really good in the wind."

Entering the Championship Rose inevitably got plenty of attention, as did Sergio Garcia, the runner-up from Carnoustie and the favourite in the betting, and defending Champion Padraig Harrington. Garcia, the Players champion, scored 72 but never worked his way into contention this year. Harrington was hardly thinking of being in contention when he teed off at 7.58am. He was thinking merely of finishing. In fact, only one other man could have been happier

Excerpts FROM THE Press

Padraig Harrington was relieved when he could hit from the rought without pain.

to be out in the worst of the wind and the rain. Heath Slocum had flown over from America as the first alternate, but when he saw Harrington warming up on the range he figured his best chance of playing in his first Open had gone.

But with half-an-hour's notice he was informed Toru Taniguchi had withdrawn and he would be teeing off alongside John Daly and Richard Finch at 9.42am. Of the three, Slocum's 73 was the best result. "I was a little stunned, because after Padraig teed off I didn't figure I had much of a chance," Slocum said. "It was like getting on a plane standby. It helped that I played two practice rounds. The R&A were very gracious and I had full playing privileges. They treated me just like I was in the tournament."

If not quite subject to as much scrutiny as Tiger's knee at the US

'There's something about this event that stimulates you,' said Greg Norman, whose 70 surprised and delighted the spectators.

Open, Harrington's right wrist was the centre of attention, both medically and in the media, on the eve of the Championship. The injury occurred on the previous Saturday evening, at around 10pm, as the Irishman swung his driver into a bean bag. This impact exercise is designed to strengthen the wrists in the same way that Henry Cotton used to swing at old car tyres. Amazing that he should be doing anything that evening considering he had just retained his Irish PGA title earlier in the day at the European Club. Harrington won the title in a playoff in 2007 before going on to beat Garcia in extra holes at Carnoustie. This time he won by four strokes from Philip Walton, having battled through weather every bit as bad as at Birkdale.

The wrist apart, Harrington's preparations were running on a similar track to 12 months earlier. His sports psychologist, Bob Rotella, was staying in his house. On the Tuesday evening he again attended the Association of Golf Writers' Annual Dinner, collecting an award for his Open win. Harrington's 2008 season to date was solid but not spectacular, perhaps best illustrated by the fact that he was not yet assured of a place in the European Ryder Cup team for the match at

Bart Bryant birdied No 18 for 70.

1

Round of the Day

OFFICIAL SCORECARD
THE OPEN CHAMPIONSHIP 2008
Royal Birkdale

Graeme McDOWELL
Game 32
Thursday 17 July at 12:36 pm

FOR R&A USE ONLY 32.2

ROUND 1
18 HOLE TOTAL

THIS ROUND 69

69

VERIFIED NM

ROUND 1

Hole	1	2	3	4	5	6	7	8	9	Out
Yards	450	421	451	201	346	499	178	457	414	3417
Par	4	4	4	3	4	4	3	4	4	34
Score	4	4	4	3	4	5	3	4	4	35

Hole	10	11	12	13	14	15	16	17	18	In	Total
Yards	408	436	184	499	201	544	439	572	473	3756	7173
Par	4	4	3	4	3	5	4	5	4	36	70
Score	4	4	3	4	3	5	4	4	3	34	69

Signature of Marker

Signature of Competitor
Graeme McDowell

Two years after leading the first round at Royal Liverpool, Graeme McDowell took advantage of better weather in the afternoon and was again in front as the joint leader with Rocco Mediate and Robert Allenby.

McDowell had only one blemish on his card, a bogey-5 on the sixth hole. He drove into the left rough and could not advance his second shot more than 10 yards. He laid up on his third, struck a nine iron to 30 feet on his fourth, and holed the putt. McDowell missed the fairway off the tees on eight of 14 holes but was on the green in regulation 13 times, including the last eight holes.

He scored his only birdies on the last two holes. He reached the green of the par-5 17th hole with a five iron for his second shot and needed two putts from 25 feet. On the 473-yard 18th, he hit a nine iron from 158 yards to 12 feet.

"I was happy the way I plodded my way around the golf course today," McDowell said. "Obviously I felt very fortunate with the draw (12.36pm). The guys this morning looked like they had a really, really tough time out there in the wind and rain, and we couldn't have had it much better.

"We just had wind to deal with all day. It was blowing hard, but like I say, you can always handle one or the other, wind or rain, but together it is a pretty tough combo. I felt fortunate to get some good scoring conditions."

Low Scores

Low First Nine

Adam Scott	33
Peter Hanson	33

Low Second Nine

Robert Allenby	32

Low Round

Rocco Mediate	69
Graeme McDowell	69
Robert Allenby	69

Robert Karlsson posted 75 after an outward 35.

While struggling to 77, Oliver Wilson found the rough on No 7.

Valhalla in September. Nick Faldo, Europe's captain, was at the same dinner and could not resist issuing an instruction: "Padraig, it's time to pull your finger out."

Before he could do anything with his fingers he had to get the wrist right. He had played nine holes in practice on Tuesday, but after two shots on the 10th on Wednesday he retreated to the physiotherapy unit for more treatment. Later he simply walked the back nine. That evening his physiotherapist, Dale Richardson, convinced Harrington that he could do no more damage and the decision was made to play whatever the pain. There were a few twinges while warming up on the practice range, but the real test would be playing out of the rough.

That test would come at the very first hole after a pushed tee shot. A bogey followed and there were more visits to the rough than he would have liked on the opening few holes, but even that turned out to be a positive. "I was apprehensive going onto the course about hitting from the rough," he said. "Of course, that's what I managed to do over the first four or five holes, but when it didn't hurt I started to become more relaxed. After seven or eight holes I wasn't thinking about it at all."

Two over after a bogey at the fourth, Harrington hit his approach close at the fifth to get a shot back,

and though he bogeyed the sixth, again he holed from three feet for a birdie at the eighth. "It was a big course today," he said. "You have to have a number of breaks to help you through a tough day. I holed a long putt from 30 feet at the second for a par and got up and down from 50 yards at the next. Then I hit my first good shot at the fifth, really close, and took advantage. Those things keep you going."

He was still only two over when he got to the last two holes, but here his lack of practice hurt him. He found the left rough off the 17th tee and ended up with a bogey-6 and bogeyed the last after driving into a bunker on the right. "Obviously, the bogey-bogey finish has tainted the round a little bit, but 74 will be a respectable enough score with

❶

His umbrella a windscreen, Retief Goosen battled to 71 with four birdies.

54 holes to go in this tournament," he said. "My wrist is only going to get better. There would only be a slim chance that I wouldn't be able to complete the tournament."

A score of 74, four over, was perhaps under the effective par of the morning. It was Harrington's playing companion Retief Goosen who set the clubhouse lead with 71, only to be matched by Mike Weir, who teed off 90 minutes later. Goosen, after a three-week tournament break resting up and practising at home, recovered from a double bogey at the fifth to get under par with his third birdie of the day at the short 14th. At the ninth he almost holed out with a six iron, while on the par-3 12th he hit the flagstick with a five iron. He missed a short par putt at the 15th to set up a bogey, bogey, birdie, bogey finish. It was perhaps the finest round of the day given the conditions for most of it and one he would have taken after being

Trevor Immelman was on 74 with birdies on the two par-5s.   **Mike Weir posted 71 despite playing in the morning.**

woken up by the rain at 2am. "The ball was going absolutely nowhere in that wind. It was hard," he said.

Goosen and Weir, who claimed the first eagle of the week at the 17th when he holed from 15 feet to offset one of his two double bogeys, were the only two players of the 14 at 71 or better who played in the morning. Choi and Ian Poulter, who was driven on by the thought of a cup of tea and a piece of cake, were the only ones at 72 playing in the morning, although the weekend's final leaderboard turned out to be well populated with those unfortunates on the "early-late" side of the draw.

But there was no getting away from the fact that the three co-leaders all played in the afternoon. "I sat at home this morning at breakfast with my cereal and a cup of coffee and thought, 'God, do I really have to go out there this afternoon?'" McDowell said. "The guys this morning looked like they had a really, really tough time. We just had the wind blowing, and you can usually handle one or the other, wind or rain, but both is a pretty tough combo."

Full of confidence after the biggest win of his career, McDowell was hoping to make a better finish to his campaign than two years earlier when he had led at Hoylake on the opening day. "I felt like a

It's a **Fact**

Adam Scott was the only player to reach two under par in the first round when he scored a birdie on the 15th hole. Scott then took bogeys on the next two holes to finish on level-par 70. There were 15 others who reached one under par at some point of the first round. They were Tom Watson, KJ Choi, Shintaro Kai, Retief Goosen, Robert Karlsson, Angel Cabrera, Anthony Kim, Peter Hanson, Anthony Wall, Douglas McGuigan, Alex Cejka, Peter Appleyard and — the three co-leaders of the first round — Rocco Mediate, Graeme McDowell, and Robert Allenby — those last three with birdies on both the 17th and 18th holes.

Sergio Garcia said of his 72, 'It was not as tough as this morning, but it was difficult.'

Ian Poulter returned his 72 in the morning conditions.

rabbit in the headlights two years ago," he admitted. "Then I didn't have the belief in my game I do now. Today you knew it was going to be a battle for survival, and my attitude was it was going to be 18 little challenges where par was a great score on every hole." He succeeded in 17 of those 18 challenges, better than anyone else in the field, only dropping a shot at the sixth where his second shot in the rough travelled only four yards. His patience was rewarded when he found the green at the 17th in two and made a 4 and then hit a nine iron to 12 feet at the last to join Mediate on 69.

The American had been playing only two groups in front and at three over after five holes was not faring so well. But he played the last 13 holes in four under, chipping in from left of the 17th green and then holing a 20-footer at the last. The explanation for his score was actually simple — he

Mediate Refuses To Back Off

If you had seen Rocco Mediate on the 10th fairway on the Sunday before The Open began, you would not have put any money on him making it to the first tee for a second practice round, never mind anything more ambitious.

At that moment on that sunny afternoon, Mediate was flat on his back receiving treatment from Cindi Hilfman, his personal therapist, for a sacroiliac that has been troubling him for years. After a few minutes he got up, took a few steps rather gingerly, made a swing or two, and off he went, temporarily patched up.

But even if you had not seen this, you would not have put much money on Mediate, despite his gutsy performance in taking Tiger Woods to the 91st hole of the US Open the previous month. At 45 Mediate has been unable to play a full schedule for nearly three years because of his back, and when he did compete you could see he was in some discomfort from the way he stretched and contorted himself as often as he could.

Mediate had not won a tournament for six years, and when he played these days Hilfman followed him each round to administer any on-course treatment. What he really needed was to take one year off and rehabilitate his back, but that was not possible. Beware the injured golfer is one thing. Beware a middle-aged man who is overweight and has a back that cannot last 18 holes without treatment, surely that is another.

So by rights on Thursday, Mediate should have been blown into the Irish Sea by winds gusting up to 35mph and soaked to the skin by rain squalls that hit Royal Birkdale with the ferocity of a monsoon. He was lucky in that he was slightly removed from the eye of the storm. Those who started between the first tee-off time of 6.30 and 11.52 got the worst of it. Mediate, Paul Lawrie, the 1999 Open Champion, and Angel Cabrera, the 2007 US Open champion, teed off at 12.14.

What happened then is this. On the day when the field averaged 75.973 and major champions such as Ernie Els, Vijay Singh, and John Daly went round in 80, Mediate went round in 69, one under par, one of only three sub-par rounds. Two over par after 12 holes, he covered the remaining six holes in three under, coming home in 33. He holed more putts in the five- to 12-foot range than usual. He holed one of 40 feet on the 13th for a birdie, one of 15 feet on the 18th for another birdie, and on the 17th he chipped in from well off the green.

The usual on-course medical repair work could have begun on the fifth where Mediate told Hilfman that he felt "absolutely miserable. I can't move." But it was not until the 11th hole that Hilfman was brought into action, this time treating her patient by the side of the 11th green for 30 seconds.

What to make of Mediate? Was he a man inspired by performing so well against Woods? "I think the duel with Tiger has done nothing but make me better even though I did not win the tournament," Mediate said. "Yeah, he's the best player in the world, but that's what you want to go up against. I'd like to do it every week."

What to make of this round? "I have no explanation whatsoever," Mediate said, laughing. "I have no idea why that happened. … I would have been ecstatic with 73 or 74 today."

—John Hopkins

Mediate could not begin to explain why he was playing so well.

First Round Scores	
Players Below Par	3
Players At Par	3
Players Above Par	148

Round One Hole Summary

HOLE	PAR	YARDS	EAGLES	BIRDIES	PARS	BOGEYS	D.BOGEYS	HIGHER	RANK	AVERAGE
1	4	450	0	5	67	68	14	2	2	4.622
2	4	421	0	5	73	64	12	2	3	4.577
3	4	451	0	7	105	41	3	0	11	4.256
4	3	201	0	19	92	44	1	0	15	3.173
5	4	346	0	18	84	48	5	1	10	4.276
6	4	499	0	4	38	88	23	3	1	4.891
7	3	178	0	11	93	47	5	0	8	3.295
8	4	457	0	9	112	27	7	1	12	4.224
9	4	414	0	14	102	33	5	2	13	4.224
OUT	34	3417	0	92	766	460	75	11		37.538
10	4	408	0	10	76	58	7	4	6	4.497
11	4	436	0	4	75	61	13	1	4	4.558
12	3	184	0	12	94	41	7	0	9	3.279
13	4	499	0	11	100	41	2	0	14	4.221
14	3	201	0	7	98	46	2	1	7	3.299
15	5	544	0	28	89	30	6	1	17	5.110
16	4	439	0	5	76	61	9	3	5	4.539
17	5	572	2	60	62	25	5	0	18	4.812
18	4	473	0	18	100	35	1	0	16	4.123
IN	36	3756	2	155	770	398	52	10		38.438
TOTAL	70	7173	2	247	1536	858	127	21		75.976

Even after 80, Vijay Singh said he did not play badly. The other two players in his group, Hunter Mahan and Amateur champion Reinier Saxton, were on the same score.

Peter Appleyard led The Open — 'I hope someone got a photograph' — Yes, indeed.

needed only 21 putts. "I made pretty much every single putt I could have made today," he said. By contrast, Allenby was the man who hit most greens in regulation — 15 of them — and after going out in 37 came home with the day's best 32. At the 17th he just missed his eagle putt from 10 feet, but slotted home a 20-footer at the last for his fourth birdie. While others had birdied the first, or an early hole, to get on the leaderboard, these three never led until their 3s at the last.

Of those 16 players who got under par, the one who was there longest was Adam Scott, while the last of them was Peter Appleyard. The 30 year-old club professional from Kent teed off in the day's last group and birdied the third hole before suffering a double bogey at the sixth on the way to 74. "To be joint leader for a couple of holes is something I'll take for the rest of my life," he said. "I hope someone got a photograph."

Scott was the only player all week to reach the dizzying heights of two under par. He did so by claiming one of the day's more extraordinary birdies at the sixth hole, one of only four, and then birdieing the 15th. No one else had got beyond the sixth hole without dropping a shot, and then only European Open winner Ross Fisher, but Scott got all the way to the 16th before a three-putt meant his first bogey. He also bogeyed the next to finish on 70 when perhaps he deserved to be leading. "It's a shame, but overall it was pretty positive stuff," said the Australian.

Excerpts FROM THE Press

"Ever play golf in a car wash? Wish you could hit four irons in a wind tunnel?"
—**Gene Wojciehowski, ESPN.com**

"Among those who suffered most was the world No 2, Phil Mickelson, who is all but out of contention already after a nine-over 79 which included a triple-bogey 7 at the sixth after he lost his ball. Ernie Els and Vijay Singh, two others who might have hoped to take advantage of Tiger Woods's absence, both failed to break 80."
—**Lawrence Donegan, *The Guardian***

"Cindi Hilfman began to understand Rocco Mediate's new life the week after the US Open. Hilfman, whose work as Mediate's physical therapist helped him resuscitate his sagging career, was sitting in a Starbucks in Los Angeles, waiting for Mediate. She watched a parade of customers recognize the journeyman golfer and 'fight over' who would buy his coffee. 'He's like a rock star now,' Hilfman said. 'It's totally weird.'"
—**Ron Kroichick,
*San Francisco Chronicle***

"Nick Dougherty emerged from a windswept Royal Birkdale last night with his Open dream still intact. The Liverpool golfer produced a gutsy performance over the closing holes to claw his way back from a potentially damaging position with two birdies in four holes."
—**Richard Williamson,
*Liverpool Daily Post***

John Daly pitched close enough on No 12 to make par, a rare save in his 10-over-par round.

Ernie Els's 80 was his worst score ever in The Open.

Australia's strong showing on the Birkdale roll of honour was looking a good omen. Allenby played a practice round with Ian Baker-Finch when he teed up as an amateur in the 1991 Open. That year's Champion walked part of Allenby's Wednesday practice round here. "I got a lot of knowledge from Finchy about his win, although the course has changed a lot," Allenby said. Norman finished in the top 10 in 1991 and in the top 20 in 1983, but the Great White Shark had not played in a major championship since The Open in 2005. A successful businessman who at 53 had made only limited appearances on the senior circuits, he arrived in Southport with the Senior Open Championship at Royal Troon the following week more on his mind.

Norman had been practising at Skibo Castle, but before that had been on honeymoon in the Bahamas with his new birdie, the former tennis champion Chris Evert. His 70, to sit alongside those of Scott and American Bart Bryant, received a warm reception from the gallery at the 18th green. But he couldn't keep it up, could he?

Second Time Around

A different McDowell shared the top of the leaderboard

By Mike Aitken

Before Graeme McDowell emerged as the surprise first-round leader of The Open at Hoylake in 2006, the Ulsterman went in a local hostelry in search of cool refreshment. While McDowell was enjoying a supp of beer, a stranger approached. McDowell was expecting to be asked for an autograph. Instead, the man said: "You get it pretty laid off at the top, don't you? Get a bit of work done on that, will you?"

Two years later at Royal Birkdale and McDowell again straddled the top of The Open leaderboard after the first 18 holes, matching the low score of 69 set by Robert Allenby and Rocco Mediate. The changes in his on-course demeanour, as well as his swing, however, meant that McDowell no longer had to put up with listening to punters in pubs offer advice about a hitch in his action. He knew he had done the work.

McDowell had arrived in Southport as the winner of the Barclays Scottish Open at Loch Lomond on the Sunday before The Open began, as well as the Ballantine's Championship in March. A Ryder Cup player in waiting, McDowell's emergence as one of Europe's most consistent young golfers could be attributed to the improved technique of an outstanding ball striker.

At Loch Lomond, for example, McDowell, 28 years of age, had defeated a stellar field which included Phil Mickelson, Ernie Els, and Adam Scott, banking the winner's cheque largely because he found more greens in regulation than any other player. Precision was the key to his success in Scotland and no disadvantage on a blustery afternoon in Southport either.

He only made one error on the daunting sixth hole when he found the left

rough off the tee. Full of confidence after the most significant win of his career, the Irishman was a touch greedy and only advanced his ball around 10 yards or so. Once he eventually escaped from the long grass, McDowell chipped to 30 feet from the pin and holed the bogey putt. "That," he recalled later, "was really big for my momentum."

Although conditions were not quite as

brutal for those who played in the afternoon as the morning starters, it was still a three-club wind in which McDowell needed to reach for a four iron to move the ball 170 yards. But at least it wasn't as miserably wet. "I would be the first to admit that," he said. "I sat at home this morning with my breakfast cereal and cup of coffee in my hand going, 'God, do I really have to go out there this afternoon?' Obviously we got pretty lucky. Generally I didn't have my (rain) jacket on all day. We can count ourselves very fortunate. It's not often the 4.30 tee time at The Open is a good draw, but the guys out there earlier had it even tougher than we did."

Nothing became McDowell's round quite like the closing flourish. He found the sloping green of the par-5 17th with a five iron and made a two-putt birdie. Even more impressive was the piercing nine iron to the

last green and a 12-foot putt for birdie. It was a stroke which meant he emerged as one of only three players in the field of 156 to better par on the first day.

This was evidence of how much McDowell had progressed since 2006. Once a top college player in America and a Walker Cup stalwart, McDowell won the 2002 Scandinavian Masters in only his fourth appearance on the European Tour.

He won the Italian Open in 2004 and placed sixth on the Order of Merit. McDowell, however, struggled between 2005 and 2007. "It didn't take me long to realise that it's pretty tough out here," he admitted.

As to that previous appearance in the media centre at a major championship, McDowell recalled: "Yeah, I certainly felt like a rabbit in the headlights a couple years ago at Hoylake. I was like, what's this all about? But I've been face to face with you guys quite a lot in the last few weeks. There's a comfort level which helps you to deal with (that situation), move on and get ready to play again. I certainly feel like quite a different player than I was two years ago. Then, I didn't really have a whole lot of belief in my game and it caught up with me on the weekend.

"As I've said, it was a time when I lacked belief in my swing and couldn't really string four rounds together. Obviously I've been showing some form for the last 10 to 12 months, (finding) consistency, really punching in some rounds, and certainly stringing four rounds together. I've got more belief in my game and what I'm doing now. I'm a lot more comfortable in this position than I was two years ago."

Still The Australian Hero

By Andy Farrell

Norman in a romantic comeback, but Choi steals the halfway lead.

For much of the day, after he holed an improbable birdie putt from 45 feet on the first green at breakfast time, a 53 year-old businessman who plays more tennis than golf led The 137th Open Championship. But then Greg Norman is a two-time former Open Champion, and all the old instincts started flooding back to the extent that by lunchtime he was the clubhouse leader. It was only around suppertime that KJ Choi stole in with 67 to take the halfway lead at one under par, but by then Royal Birkdale was awash in nostalgia for an era when the game's greatest predator was a Shark rather than a Tiger.

And, in any case, who can resist a love story? A month before Norman had married Chris Evert, the former tennis champion, winner of three Wimbledon titles and 18 majors in all. "My life is great," Norman said. "I feel great. I have a wonderful wife, my whole being is just beautiful. I enjoy playing golf, I enjoy spending time at home with Chrissie and my kids. I enjoy my business and what I'm doing. It's the first time I've got the most beautiful balance in my life."

The honeymoon took in the Bahamas, then a little golf at Skibo Castle in Scotland, and now Birkdale. "For the last month my mind has been elsewhere," he continued. "We had a lot of preparations for the wedding and had a great time over there. The least of my worries was getting out there practising and getting ready for the Open. My expectations were almost nil coming in. So, of course, it feels like stepping back in time. But my expectations are still realistically low. I have to be that way.

"My mind still salivates about playing golf. When I come back from a practice session after a couple of hours I feel great. But after all the surgeries I've had in the last few years, my body doesn't want to practise. I don't have the physical ability to go out there and hit balls for eight, 10 hours a day as I used to. You can keep yourself physically fit, but the body doesn't react the way your mind wants it to react. The tennis I've being playing with Chris is probably the best thing for me, because it keeps me loose, it's good on the cardiovascular, it keeps my lower back strong."

Greg Norman had two rounds of 70, level par.

Waiting for Norman was new wife Chris Evert.

Woody Austin, Norman's playing companion, offered the suggestion on the 16th green that, without all the tennis with his wife, the Australian might never have been able to cope with the awkward stance for his bunker shot — one foot in, one out — and play the most sublime recovery that set up a par save. He made a mess of the 17th to drop a shot and go back to level par for the Championship, but as he walked up the 18th fairway, he received a thunderous reception, as if it was late on Sunday afternoon. He admitted it got to him a bit as he raced his long approach putt 20 feet past — the hole was located near the fall-off at the back of the green — but then he holed the one back to finish in the grand style and fully deserving of the hug from his new bride by the scorers' hut.

"I didn't let myself get down after the first putt, just trusted my stroke and stayed calm in the mind, and that's why it went in," Norman explained afterwards to a packed press conference. "But the feeling is phenomenal. The support here has been great. The adrenaline might have been running just a little bit more. Even just seeing the press room full is pretty good."

For a man brought up playing some of the finest Australian courses, Norman always had a natural affinity for links golf. "I always thought of the Open as the home of golf," he said. "At home we played a lot of bump-and-run, feel-the-shot golf, not as dramatic as this, but I've always gravitated to enjoying the game

KJ Choi had 67, three under par, with only one bogey.

"As curtain calls go, the scene unfolding amid the ancient dunes at Royal Birkdale surely would rank among the most compelling golf has seen for a very long time."

—Larry Dorman,
The New York Times

"Halfway through the 137th playing of The Open Championship, perhaps never before has the collective performance of the home players been so utterly abject. In weather hardly attractive to those from overseas — and utterly familiar to those born on these shores — only two golfers from England, Ian Poulter and Anthony Wall, played well enough to make it into the top 20 names on the leaderboard."

—John Huggan, *The Guardian*

"In the United States, Camilo Villegas has been voted one of *People* magazine's 'hottest bachelors,' a clothes-horse with a penchant for figure-hugging trousers and top. And yet there is more to him than meets the eye."

—Peter Dixon, *The Times*

"When do you start to dream, to start thinking of what it would be like to clasp the Claret Jug and hold it close to your chest? To have your name engraved next to the legends of the past, and the present? In Graeme McDowell's case, not just yet."

—Philip Reid, *Irish Times*

Four over par after 11 holes, Graeme McDowell played the last seven holes with birdie on No 16 and the rest pars.

better here. I always enjoy playing different types of shots, seeing them in my eye and the executing. Take the 10th this morning, 108 yards to the pin uphill and I'm chipping it with an eight iron. Most guys would try a pitching wedge, but once it gets above the spectators and the mound before there, the wind just knocks it down and the ball could be coming back off the green very quickly. Those are the shots you draw on from your past experiences."

Tom Watson called Norman one of the best bad weather players ever. The Shark proved it by winning the 1986 Open at Turnberry in weather that was even fouler than here. Many a Dunhill Cup appearance for Australia at St Andrews in October provided more testing experiences. On Thursday Norman had 70 and he matched the same score on Friday. After holing for birdie at the first he

was tied with the overnight leaders Rocco Mediate, Graeme McDowell, and Robert Allenby. At the sixth he tangled with the rough both left and right and took a double-bogey 6. It was but a momentary blip as he hit back with birdies at the next two holes. A four iron from 181 yards finished 25 feet away at the short seventh, while he followed that putt with another from 15 feet at the eighth. Then it was a long stretch of par golf, interrupted only by 6 at the 17th.

Conditions were better than on Thursday, with the rain coming only in squally showers and the wind not quite so strong, although still gusting to over 25mph. Again the morning starters had the worst of it, so the field was beginning to even out. Mediate was the first of the leaders onto the course and, wouldn't you know it, he played better from tee to green than the day before, but the putts

Second Round Leaders

HOLE	1	2	3	4	5	6	7	8	9	10	11	12	13	14	15	16	17	18	
PAR	4	4	4	3	4	4	3	4	4	4	4	3	4	3	5	4	5	4	TOTAL
KJ Choi	[5]	4	(3)	3	4	4	3	4	4	4	4	3	(3)	3	5	4	(4)	(3)	67-139
Greg Norman	(3)	4	4	3	4	[6]	(2)	(3)	4	4	4	3	4	3	5	4	[6]	4	70-140
Camilo Villegas	[5]	[5]	4	(2)	(3)	4	3	4	(3)	4	4	3	[5]	(2)	(4)	(3)	(4)	(3)	65-141
Rocco Mediate	4	4	4	3	4	[5]	(2)	4	4	4	[6]	3	4	[4]	5	4	[6]	(3)	73-142
Graeme McDowell	4	[5]	4	3	4	[5]	3	4	4	[5]	[5]	3	4	3	5	(3)	5	4	73-142
Jim Furyk	4	4	4	3	4	[5]	3	(3)	4	4	[5]	(2)	[5]	3	5	4	5	4	71-142
Robert Allenby	[5]	[5]	4	3	4	4	[4]	4	[5]	4	4	3	4	[4]	(4)	4	(4)	4	73-142
Alexander Noren	4	[5]	4	3	4	[5]	(2)	4	4	4	[5]	3	4	(2)	5	4	(4)	4	70-142
Padraig Harrington	4	(3)	4	3	4	[5]	3	4	4	[5]	[5]	3	4	3	(4)	4	(3)	(3)	68-142
David Duval	(3)	4	4	3	4	[5]	3	4	4	(3)	(3)	3	[5]	(2)	5	[5]	5	4	69-142
Fredrik Jacobson	4	[5]	(3)	3	(3)	4	[4]	4	4	4	4	3	4	[4]	5	[5]	5	4	72-143
Stephen Ames	[5]	(3)	4	3	4	[5]	3	(3)	4	[5]	4	[4]	4	3	(4)	4	5	(3)	70-143
Peter Hanson	(3)	4	4	[4]	4	[5]	[4]	(3)	[5]	(3)	4	3	4	3	[6]	[5]	(4)	4	72-143
Stuart Appleby	4	4	4	[4]	[5]	[5]	[4]	(3)	4	(3)	4	3	4	3	5	4	(4)	4	71-143
Ian Poulter	4	4	4	[4]	(3)	4	3	4	4	4	4	3	[5]	[4]	5	4	(4)	4	71-143

this time would not drop. He shared the lead with Norman until a double bogey at the 11th, and after 6 at the 17th, finished in style by hitting an eight iron to six inches at the last. Still, the American seemed to be basking in the glow of his challenge at the US Open and the gallery at the last responded in kind. Asked about his rapport with the crowd, Mediate said: "I love it. The roars are different over here. They're deeper. I don't know how to explain it, but it's pretty cool."

McDowell dropped out of the lead with a bogey at the second and was out in 36 and missing the rhythm of recent rounds. But by the 16th he had it back and produced a wondrous shot, a three iron from 180 yards directly into the wind to five feet. After that he just had to hole the putt. "I was looking to get something out of the last few holes and, obviously, I was ecstatic with that shot," said the man from Portrush.

Like Mediate he had scored 73 to join the American on two over par. It was a pattern that continued with Allenby doing exactly the same, this after

Phil Mickelson improved 11 strokes to 68, advancing from a tie for 123rd to a tie for 38th.

Alexander Noren, a Swede in his first Open, was on 142 with a share of fourth place.

These three players improved on their first-round scores to be on 144. Clockwise from left, they were Soren Hansen (75 to 69), Scott Verplank (77 to 67), and Jean Van de Velde (73 to 71).

Low Scores	
Low First Nine	
Anders Hansen	31
Low Second Nine	
Camilo Villegas	32
Low Round	
Camilo Villegas	65

bogeying the first two holes but as on Thursday responding on the back nine. Jim Furyk slipped in with 71 to join them on two over, the same mark as Open debutant Alexander Noren, from Sweden, whose 70 was helped by holing out of a bunker at the seventh.

But by then it was not just Norman in front of this pack. After two holes, both of which he bogeyed, Camilo Villegas was eight over par for the Championship and in danger of missing the cut. Birdies at the fourth, the fifth, and the ninth put the Colombian out in 33, but it was nothing compared to what he did after bogeying the 13th. The 26 year-old, in his third year on the PGA Tour in America but without a win, is one of the most exciting young players around, partly because of his agility in crouching down Spiderman-like to view his putts on the greens, but mainly because no one has any

In danger of missing the cut, Camilo Villegas posted 65 and climbed to third place.

In the Words of the Competitors…

"

"Honestly, there is probably less pressure on me than anybody out here, because even though I'm in the position I'm in, I'm going to go out there and just have fun with it."

—Greg Norman

"Whether it's windy or not over the weekend, I don't think it's going to matter, because the course is difficult as it is. I just have to try my best until the end."

—KJ Choi

"Very interesting. I obviously played unbelievable."
—Camilo Villegas

"It was tough again. But I'm very happy. It was a good day and if it wasn't for the couple of blemishes, I could have been under par."

—Jean Van de Velde

"It's a bit disappointing not to play better. I struggled with the swing and the putting. I got the better side of the draw and didn't take full advantage of that."

—Adam Scott

"I've been struggling for years with my back, and to be able to do this in this weather is marvellous."

—Rocco Mediate

"

David Duval

Rediscovering His Greatness

Of recent American winners of The Open, few have been as popular as David Duval. It is as if the moment Duval took off his sunglasses at his victory speech after the 2001 Open he revealed himself the way he really is. To some of the most knowledgeable and enthusiastic golf fans in the world he was not an inscrutable American any more, not the man who hid behind sunglasses, the man whose eyes they couldn't see. He was baring his soul to them and they liked him for doing that. And then when he spoke so well in victory while cradling the Claret Jug, caressing it with his words, then they liked him even more.

Duval had endured a fairly wretched time since then, but now he seemed a different person, and it didn't take long for him to prove that this was indeed the case. He might have missed 10 out of 12 cuts in the US and withdrawn from the 11th event, but 73 in the first round when the weather was at its worst reminded us that he still had the skills that had once made him the No 1 golfer in the world.

"I am a big fan of this Championship," Duval said. "I think they set it up exactly as you would want a tournament to be set up. It's set up for weather, and if you don't get wind and rain, then you can see eight-under, 10-under, and 12-under-par scores win the golf tournament. But if you get that weather and the wind, the element that is ever elusive in this golf tournament, then the golf course presents tremendous challenges."

It got better. In the second round, Duval's 69 was one of 12 scores below par, and far from missing the cut, which fell at nine over par, he sailed past it. He was one of seven men on 142, three strokes behind KJ Choi, the halfway leader.

"For you guys writing, it's a funny story, a little different, I agree," Duval said, trying to explain why he could appear to play so badly in the US and do so well in Britain. "But I've said when I've been asked this year that I'm playing a lot better than my results have shown. I was very pleased with how I played last week in Moline. So I came over here feeling quite good about my golf despite coming off another missed cut."

There was more to it than that, however. Also contributing to Duval's good form was the way he was made to feel someone special by the spectators. Used to fans who said to themselves: "What's the matter with Duval?" he found himself playing golf in front of spectators who were willing him on. "I've felt it every year I've played since (2001). Open Champions are embraced forever. The fact that I have struggled a lot since then and am slowly getting things back to where I'd like them to be, I think they appreciate the hard work. You are talking about golfers and true golf fans here. They play the game. They understand it. They know the work it takes and they know I've had to work at it for some time."

—John Hopkins

'I don't feel as though I'm stepping back in time, back to 2001,' David Duval said. 'I am looking to the future. I'm looking foward to playing great golf from here until my early or mid 40s. That is what I am striving for.'

Sharing the lead until taking double bogey here at No 11, Rocco Mediate finished with 73.

idea what he is about to do next. Here he finished with five birdies in a row.

It was an astonishing sequence of golf that could not have been imagined in the brutal conditions of Thursday and would still have been breathtaking had it been a balmy, still, perfect day, which it was not. He started by hitting a five iron to 16 feet at the short 14th and holed the putt. Turning into the wind at the par-5 15th, Villegas pulled his drive into the rough on the left, but the lie was good enough to get a three wood at it. The recovery just cleared the cross bunkers, and from there he chipped up a low nine iron to six feet for the pitch-and-putt birdie.

The 16th was now playing as the third hardest hole on the course, after the 11th and the sixth, but he hit a beautiful drive, followed by a low five iron that ran 17 feet past the hole. "I hit a good putt, but I thought it wasn't going to break enough at the end," Villegas said. "It just snuck in on the right side."

Now Villegas turned with the wind at his back for the par-5 17th, and after another fine drive only had a seven-iron approach shot. "But man, that's a funky green and it's tough to hit," he said. The

> ## It's a
> # Fact
>
> The 65 by Camilo Villegas was two strokes off the lowest score ever for The Open Championship at Royal Birkdale. That was the 63 by Jodie Mudd in the fourth round of 1991, and that shares the Championship record with six others. There have been four rounds of 64 at Royal Birkdale — by Craig Stadler (1983), Graham Marsh (1991), Fred Couples (1991), Ian Baker-Finch (1991). Other rounds of 65 were by Tiger Woods and John Huston, both in 1998.

Choi's Major Chance

Well-regarded Korean player seeks to be first Asian Champion

KJ Choi arrived at Royal Birkdale as the man most likely to do what no Asian golfer had done before him: win a major championship.

That notion appeared less fanciful when he stepped off the 18th green after the second round. Choi had just posted a three-under-par 67 to lead The Open. Although he began the round with a bogey on the opening hole, Choi didn't put a foot wrong over the next 17 holes. He birdied the third and 13th, then ended the round with two birdies to signal that this might be the year of the East.

Choi's score not only led The Open, it marked his lowest in 28 rounds in his ninth appearance in the game's oldest championship.

"Today was probably the best round I've ever played in the Open," Choi said. "Today all my shots — the swing, the putting, everything — worked the way I wanted it to."

It also marked another watershed for the solid Korean. "I don't think I've ever led in a major. With the experiences of playing in numerous other majors before, I think the key thing that I've learned is to stay patient."

Choi had a little help on his way to the top of the leaderboard. He had Andy Prodger on his bag. Prodger is one of the most experienced caddies in the game. He won two majors with Nick Faldo, the 1987 Open Championship and 1989 Masters.

"Andy is like my big brother," Choi said. "He's like an uncle at times. He just makes me feel very relaxed and comfortable out there. We make a very good team."

Choi's name at the top of the heap didn't surprise anyone, although unlike many others in the field he probably didn't spend his childhood dreaming of winning The Open Championship.

The son of a rice farmer, Choi grew up on the island of Wando, just off the Korean coast. There were no golf courses on the

island when KJ was growing up. He spent his early teens concentrating on weightlifting before a high school golf coach introduced him to the game at a local driving range.

He turned professional in 1994, played in Korea, Japan, Asia, and Europe in the early years of his career. He tried for his PGA Tour card in 1999 and has never looked back. Despite his humble beginnings, Choi has notched up seven PGA Tour victories. He arrived in Southport as the winner of the Sony Open in Hawaii and a good bet to add The Open to his list of accomplishments.

Choi said: "If I were to win this, the reaction back in Korea would be tremendous. I know there's a lot of people that are praying for me back home."

With two rounds to go that seemed a very good possibility.

—**Alistair Tait**

Choi finished with a birdie on No 18.

ball bounced left and finished in the bunker, but he came out to three feet and holed that for his fourth birdie in a row.

Against the wishes of his caddie, Villegas stayed with the driver for his tee shot at the last. It found the left rough and not a good lie. He had 176 yards to the hole and elected to take a pitching wedge. "That tells you how funky it is to play golf around here," he said. "Obviously, I don't mean funky in a bad way." Villegas was playing in his first Open, but had previously played in two Amateur Championships, at Hoylake and Royal County Down, and was another to be inspired by the original form of the game. His second shot came out a little hotter than he was expecting, but it was dead on line, clattered into the flagstick, and finished 25 feet away. "I said to my caddie we just got a little lucky there, but let's take advantage," he said. "I rolled in a nice one." Of course he did.

Villegas had just scored 65, after 76 on Thursday, for a one-over-par total, one behind Norman. The 11-stroke difference was made up entirely on the greens: he had 34 putts in round one, 23 in round two.

Steve Stricker followed his opening 77 with 71.

"I got off to a bad start, but somehow just hung in there," he said. "You have to grind on every single shot. I love playing in these conditions, I love the fact you have to use your imagination." It did no harm that he had a practice round with Norman on Tuesday. "We talked about many things to do with links golf. He had some good advice. When somebody like that tells you something, you had better listen."

Adam Scott, who has benefited from plenty of Norman's advice over the years, and even inherited his old caddie, Tony Navarro, was not quite so inspired, although it was not for the lack of effort. "I was trying to get myself up there so I could maybe play with him over the weekend," Scott said. "That would have been awesome. He is still the Australian hero. It doesn't matter how he is playing, he knows how to get the ball round no matter what."

Scott slipped back to 74 and four over par, while Sergio Garcia's mind seemed to be elsewhere as he missed a short par putt at the last, so his 73 put him back at five over. Still not out of it, but the vibes from the Spaniard's putter were not encouraging. Thrilled to be on the same mark, however, was Chris Wood, a 20 year-old amateur from Long Ashton. Short of the green in the left rough at the

Anders Hansen (top) improved 10 strokes to 68; Stewart Cink (middle) missed the cut after a second 75; Adam Scott (bottom) slipped to 74 for a 144 total.

Excerpts
FROM
THE Press

"In the end, the putter was slammed in vain. But it did serve as an exclamation point to Ernie Els's frustration. Missing a six-foot putt as he bogeyed the 18th hole and finished the second round at one-under-par 69, the three-time major champion was at nine-over 149 and presumed he was on the way out, a victim of the cut at an Open for the first time since 1989."

—**Jim McCabe,** *The Boston Globe*

"The battle for the Silver Medal awarded to The Open's leading amateur will be an all-England affair after Bristol's Chris Wood and Maidstone's Thomas Sherreard both made the cut."

—**Tom Cary,** *The Daily Telegraph*

"Jean Van de Velde will forever be held in the affections of British sporting public after his traumas at Carnoustie in 1999. So it has been good to see him back in action here, and not too far from contention after 71 put him on four over par overall."

—**Nick Harris,** *The Independent*

"Greg Norman is not the only former No 1 player and Open Champion whose game has taken a sharp turn for the better with the elements taking a turn for the worse at Royal Birkdale. Who was that Friday evening walking purposely down the 18th fairway with his familiar name back on the leaderboard but David Duval?"

—**Christopher Clarey,** *International Herald Tribune*

Level par on the second nine, Colin Montgomerie finished on 148 to make the cut.

Amateurs Thomas Sherreard (left) and Chris Wood were playing for the Silver Medal.

Round of the Day

OFFICIAL SCORECARD
THE OPEN CHAMPIONSHIP 2008
Royal Birkdale

Camilo VILLEGAS ✓

Game 7
Friday 18 July at 7:36 am

FOR R&A USE ONLY 7.3

18 HOLE TOTAL	76
THIS ROUND	65
36 HOLE TOTAL	141

ROUND 2
36 HOLE TOTAL: 141

VERIFIED

ROUND 2

Hole	1	2	3	4	5	6	7	8	9	Out
Yards	450	421	451	201	346	499	178	457	414	3417
Par	4	4	4	3	4	4	3	4	4	34
Score	5	5	4	2	3	4	3	4	3	33

	10	11	12	13	14	15	16	17	18	In	Total
	408	436	184	499	201	544	439	572	473	3756	7173
	4	4	3	4	3	5	4	5	4	36	70
	4	4	3	5	2	4	3	4	3	32	65

Signature of Marker

Signature of Competitor — Camilo Villegas

Requiring just nine putts on the inward nine, and scoring birdies on the last five holes, young Colombian Camilo Villegas scored the low round of the week, five-under-par 65 on the second day, improving by 11 strokes on his opening card and climbing from joint 74th to third place.

"Thirty-four putts yesterday. I had 23 today, so it was an awful putting round yesterday and an unbelievable putting round today," Villegas said.

On the par-3 14th, Villegas struck a five iron to 16 feet from the hole. He drove badly on the par-5 15th and was lucky to have a good lie. He hit a three wood and then a chip to six feet. He hit lovely drives on the next two holes. Villegas took a five iron on the par-4 16th and bounced his second shot onto the green, 17 feet from the hole. His seven-iron second shot on the par-5 17th took an odd bounce into a bunker. He came out to three feet from the hole for his fourth successive birdie.

On the par-4 closing hole, Villegas took a driver against his caddie's advice and hit into a poor lie in the left rough. With 176 yards to the hole, he aimed to bounce his pitching wedge about five yards short of the green and let it roll. The shot went farther than intended but was stopped when it hit the flagstick, leaving Villegas a makeable putt.

---

last, a little nearer than where Justin Rose was on the final day in 1998, Wood holed his pitch shot. The stands were not quite full, but still there was a sudden and thrilling roar, not least thanks to the 50-odd supporters who had come up from Bristol to support the youngster.

"I fancied holing a chip shot, but it probably came at the right time," Wood said. "I probably pitched it a yard short of where I wanted to, but it ran straight into the hole. I was so aware of going long and it going off the green. To finish like that was something special. The support I had all the way round was fantastic." At five over, Wood was one shot ahead of the other amateur to make the cut, Thomas Sherreard from Chart Hills in Kent, so an intriguing duel was on for the Silver Medal.

At the halfway stage the pair sat ahead of a number of big names, and with the cut falling at nine over par, among those to miss were

Villegas has a unique view of putting.

Scores of 72 and 74 put Anthony Kim on 146, tied for 27th.

Geoff Ogilvy was eliminated on 151 after 6 on No 16.

Even 68 couldn't keep Pat Perez from missing the cut on 150.

former Champions Paul Lawrie, Mark O'Meara, Tom Watson, and John Daly, and major winners Vijay Singh, Geoff Ogilvy, and Angel Cabrera. Ernie Els made it on the number with a 69, 11 better than on Thursday, as did Paul Casey, while Ben Curtis, with 69, and Phil Mickelson, after 68, were at seven over. With three pars, two double bogeys, and a triple in his first six holes, Colin Montgomerie was at 10 over par. He had 6s at the second and the sixth and 7 at the fifth, where he whiffed a recovery from the rough to the right of the green and then had to take an unplayable. Yet the Scot battled back, birdieing the seventh and the eighth and coming home in 36 for 75 that kept him alive at eight over.

If keeping the mistakes to a minimum was the key, then Choi was the man. He only had one bogey on his card of 67. Only Mickelson and Soren Hansen, who also broke par with 69, could say the same. Scott Verplank got alongside Hansen at four over with his own 67, but Choi's was the most beautifully controlled round and ended up with him on top of the leaderboard. His dropped shot came at the first, but from then on the Korean was immaculate. He hit a nine iron to a foot at the third to get back to level for the day and then ground out the pars. His run to the summit of the leaderboard began when he holed from 20 feet at the 13th. Then he claimed a 4 at the 17th with two putts from 30 feet and holed from 25 feet at the last to pip Norman by one.

"Today was probably my best round I've ever

A pair of 71s placed Jim Furyk (with caddie Mike Cowan) three strokes off the lead.

played in the Open," Choi said. For the first time he was leading a major championship, but the 37 year-old had been lying second to Garcia at the same stage a year before at Carnoustie, where he went on to finish tied for eighth. "Today all my shots, the swing, the putting, everything worked the way I wanted it to. I think the key now is to maintain my body condition and try to finish it out. The fan support today was wonderful. I got a lot of motivation out of that."

A former powerlifter, Choi has become a fine professional golfer, winning seven times in America. A major championship, however, still awaits the Korean nation from a male golfer. The women have led the way and only a few weeks earlier Inbee Park won the US

Ian Poulter, hitting to the green on No 18, was on 143 after two rounds.

Round Two Hole Summary

HOLE	PAR	YARDS	EAGLES	BIRDIES	PARS	BOGEYS	D.BOGEYS	HIGHER	RANK	AVERAGE
1	4	450	0	14	85	48	6	1	5	4.318
2	4	421	0	9	102	38	4	1	6	4.266
3	4	451	0	22	119	12	1	0	17	3.948
4	3	201	0	10	109	35	0	0	12	3.162
5	4	346	0	25	105	19	3	2	16	4.039
6	4	499	0	2	65	73	12	2	1	4.662
7	3	178	0	14	99	38	2	1	8	3.201
8	4	457	0	18	112	21	3	0	15	4.058
9	4	414	0	18	92	39	4	1	7	4.214
OUT	**34**	**3417**	**0**	**132**	**888**	**323**	**35**	**8**		**35.868**
10	4	408	0	17	95	38	3	1	10	4.195
11	4	436	0	8	77	52	14	3	2	4.526
12	3	184	0	11	111	28	3	1	11	3.175
13	4	499	0	7	89	52	5	1	4	4.390
14	3	201	0	12	100	41	1	0	9	3.201
15	5	544	0	30	88	26	8	2	14	5.130
16	4	439	0	7	75	62	8	2	3	4.500
17	5	572	2	69	64	18	1	0	18	4.656
18	4	473	0	14	109	27	4	0	13	4.136
IN	**36**	**3756**	**2**	**175**	**808**	**344**	**47**	**10**		**37.909**
TOTAL	**70**	**7173**	**2**	**307**	**1696**	**667**	**82**	**18**		**73.777**

The 1999 winner, Paul Lawrie, bogeyed Nos 14, 15 and 16 to miss the cut on 150.

Other past Champions Ben Curtis (top) improved from 78 to 69, but Mark O'Meara posted 77 to miss the cut on 151.

Women's Open, exactly 10 years after being inspired to take up the game by Se Ri Pak's victory in the same championship. "If I were to win this," Choi added through his interpreter, "the reaction back in Korea would be tremendous. I know there are a lot of people praying for me back home."

Choi was not the only player to finish strongly and give the late afternoon a similar buzz to that of the morning. Inevitably, it came from Padraig Harrington. Having gone out in regulation figures of 34, the Irishman bogeyed the 10th and 11th holes to be six over par. Apart from that moment on Wednesday when he feared he would not be able to play at all, this was the time when a successful defence of his title looked most unlikely. He might not even make the cut.

At the 11th, he was in heavy rough on an upslope and in playing the recovery he let go of the club. "The club dug into the ground and it gave me a fright that it would hurt my wrist," he explained. "There was a good bit of jarring, but the fact that my wrist wasn't hurt and came through it, that was positive." Even better was the wedge to six feet at the 15th that started a finish of four under for the last four holes. At the 17th he hit a five iron onto the green and rolled in the 30-foot putt, straight up the slope and in. It was one of only two eagles at the hole all day, the other from young Englishman David Horsey. At the last, now enjoying the atmosphere afforded the

Excerpts FROM THE Press

"A grandstand finish of eagle, birdie at Royal Birkdale's 17th and 18th holes have infused massive energy and momentum into Padraig Harrington's defence of The Open Championship. And with the kind of high winds that rarely if ever worry him predicted for today, the 36 year-old Dubliner has good reason to quietly fancy his chances of retaining the Claret Jug."

—Charlie Mulqueen, *Irish Examiner*

"Halfway through the 2008 Open, Jim Furyk is hanging in there, staying close almost unnoticed."

—Art Spander, *The Daily Telegraph*

"David Duval said his desire to re-find 'greatness' inspired him onto The Open leaderboard. Due to injury and a lack of motivation, the former world No 1 has not won a tournament since lifting the Claret Jug at nearby Lytham St Anne's in 2001. But Duval defied his world ranking of 1087 to shoot one-under-par 69 to sit three shots off the halfway lead."

—Neil McLeman, *Daily Mirror*

"Aided by Andy Prodger, one of he most experienced bag men on the circuit and himself an Open winner after helping Nick Faldo to the 1987 Open, KJ Choi took advantage of the day's best conditions to card a three-under-par 67, a score bettered only by Camilo Villegas's freakish 65 earlier in the day."

—Paul Kelso, *The Guardian*

Padraig Harrington got a fright, but was not injured at No 11 on this shot.

arrival of the defending champion, Harrington hit a nine iron from 183 yards to five feet and sunk that.

"After all the hard work on Thursday and I finished bogey, bogey, to come back today and finish 3-3, I suppose it evens it up," Harrington said. "I was beginning to get worried about the cut, but the finish was much more relaxing than yesterday. You just have to wait for your chances and take them when you get them. This whole tournament is likely to be sorted out on the last nine holes and you just want to be in the hunt. If you are in the mix and do a few good things with nine holes to go, you'll be the winner."

With 68, Harrington joined the pack at two over par, three strokes behind Choi. The last man in on that mark was slightly unexpected but a welcome visitor in David Duval. The 2001 Champion lost form dramatically since his victory and this was only the second time in 2008 that he had made the halfway cut. But rounds of 73 and 69, including a chip-in for birdie at the 10th, hinted at more consistent play. His name certainly added to an intriguing leaderboard that brought a fascinating prospect for the third round. And that was even before looking at Saturday's weather forecast.

Harrington Saves Best For His Defence

By Lewine Mair

Padraig Harrington's Open triumph in 2007 was one he could not have embraced more heartily. He did everything that was asked of him by the media, TV, and everyone else, and never once blamed any of these parties for keeping him from the task in hand — namely, winning more tournaments.

When people suggested that he might have been just too generous with his time, he would not have it. Since all these so-called distractions went hand in hand with winning The Open, what was there not to like about them?

Yet when June 2008 gave way to July and he still had no wins under his belt since Carnoustie, he admitted that it was beginning to worry him. "It's been a strange year," he said. "Yes, I've had a few top-10 finishes, but that's not why I'm out here. I can't pretend that I'm working on my game with longer-term goals in mind, because I'm quite interested in short-term goals at the moment. Winning is where the focus is at."

Harrington had shortly before returned from the US Open at Torrey Pines where he finished joint 36th. The performance had not worried him until a visitor came to his Dublin front door and spoke in the hushed tones of one who had learned of a family bereavement. "What on earth happened to you?" he asked.

The visitor's attitude prompted Harrington to study his statistics which showed that but for five near-misses from 10 feet and under on the greens, he would have been touching on the top 10. "I couldn't," he said, "look at my performance and say I did much wrong. There was no reason to change anything."

If his US Open result was less than spectacular, he still learned something from the week. In the first two rounds, for example, he had been able to study Angela Cabrera as

the Argentine set about trying to defend his US Open title.

"You could see all the time how much the week meant to him," Harrington said. "He was trying ever so hard — almost too hard — to make the cut. Then, when it became clear that that was not going to

happen, he was still trying to make things respectable.

"I remember thinking to myself that he had to do all these things, but that how he was playing did not take away from what he had done in '07."

Harrington was still relating such thoughts to his impending performance in The Open when, on the Saturday night after he had won the Irish Tour's PGA championship at the European Club, he injured his right wrist while hitting against an impact bag.

The injury flared up and, when he arrived at Birkdale the following day, he suggested it was only 50-50 as to whether he would make it through all four rounds.

Prior to the Championship's start, he managed no more than nine holes of practice. For the rest of the time, he walked the course with Ronan Flood, his caddie-cum-brother-in-law, and did nothing more than a bit of chipping and putting.

Everyone waited, with baited breath, to

see how he would perform when the gun went and, in the event, his first round was a more than minor triumph — 74 in which he had been heading for 72 until he signed off with a couple of bogeys. "I kind of have to focus on the positive," he said afterwards. "There are 54 holes ahead, my wrist should be getting better and better — and I know I can improve on my last couple of holes."

Like any other golfer with an injured wrist, Harrington was so intent on keeping out of the rough that he was immediately drawn to it. However, when he got by without so much as a wince after hitting from the long stuff at the first, he was able to relax. "After seven or eight holes, I wasn't thinking about it at all," he said.

On the Friday, Harrington handed in 68, which left him three shots off the pace. This time, his finish was 3-3 as against the 6-5 of the previous day. At the 572-yard 17th, he caught the green with a three wood and a five iron before holing from all of 30 feet. As for his playing of the par-4 18th, that featured a deliciously struck nine iron which finished five feet from the flag.

His injury by now was so far in the back of his mind that he was talking of it in the past tense. "It distracted me a bit and maybe even took the pressure off me a bit," he suggested.

Harrington was comfortable with where he was after two rounds. "At two over par and three behind, I'm well in there with 36 holes to go," he said. "I believe that conditions are going to be tough tomorrow, so it's unlikely anyone is going to run away with the Championship."

He looked ahead to the last nine holes on Sunday and said that he wanted to be in a position where the kind of 3-3 finish which he had just known could really count.

Third Round

No, Really, Norman Leads

By Andy Farrell

Veteran Australian is the 54-hole leader, but the defending Champion is not blown away.

As Kipling did not quite say, but others have observed, if you can keep your head when all about you are losing theirs, then you clearly don't understand the full extent of the situation. Sometimes it is best to pretend not to, and the third round of The 137th Open Championship was one of those times. With the wind at its strongest, gusting up to 50mph at times, thinking about anything other than how to navigate a path round the links of Royal Birkdale would have been disastrous.

For Greg Norman and Padraig Harrington, focusing, as the old clichés demand, on one shot at a time and seeing where they ended up was perhaps the key to surviving a bruising day on the links. And it worked. For Norman ended up, at the age of 53, as the oldest leader ever in an Open Championship and topping the 54-hole leaderboard for the eighth time in his major career. And Harrington,

---

Greg Norman posted 72, saving par on the fifth hole.

having overcome the worry of his wrist, had put himself into position to become the first European for more than 100 years to defend The Open title. Had either of them contemplated these feats prior to being assailed by interviews after their rounds, then their dreams, too, could have been blown all over the Lancashire coast.

Earlier in the week the forecast for Saturday had suggested it would be the best day of the Championship. By Thursday this had changed. By Friday night it was almost certain that the third round would be one of extreme survival. And by 2pm the wind was up to at least 30mph and gusting far more strongly. It was warmer and dry, at least, but it was a nagging, tugging wind that at any moment could wrench anything not securely planted in the ground from its moorings, like the flag on the fifth green, Phil Mickelson's cap and, after one shot, the tall, but lean, Simon Wakefield.

Under the circumstances, The R&A's course set-up team decided not only to place the hole locations on the flatter parts of the greens but to move forward the tees at three holes. The tee at the sixth went forward 13 yards and remained a monster par-4.

3

High winds resulted in a delay of play, but not a suspension.

Balls were moving on some greens.

But at the 11th and the 16th holes the reductions were 78 yards and 68 yards respectively because no other tee was available, and these holes, though not without their difficulties, lost some of their teeth. Another change was in the direction of the wind, quartering around midday to come from the northwest and altering the challenge once again.

There was one moment when it looked as if play would have to be suspended and it came with the final twoball of Norman and KJ Choi, the halfway leader, waiting to play from the first tee. Balls were moving on the greens, especially at the eighth and the 10th, where Anthony Kim's rolled eight feet away when he replaced it after marking and cleaning. There was a considerable delay but no suspension.

The 10th hole saw another problem when Fredrik Jacobson's ball was moving in a bunker on a patch of hardpan where the sand had blown away. The Swede could see his ball moving and was concerned about getting in the bunker, as there was a risk of being penalised if the ball then moved after he had taken his stance. Finally, Jacob-

Third Round Leaders

HOLE	1	2	3	4	5	6	7	8	9	10	11	12	13	14	15	16	17	18	
PAR	4	4	4	3	4	4	3	4	4	4	4	3	4	3	5	4	5	4	TOTAL
Greg Norman	5	4	5	3	4	5	3	3	4	6	4	3	4	2	5	4	4	4	72-212
Padraig Harrington	4	5	4	3	3	4	2	5	4	4	5	5	4	3	4	5	4	4	72-214
KJ Choi	4	4	4	3	4	6	3	5	4	6	4	3	3	3	6	4	5	4	75-214
Simon Wakefield	4	4	4	4	4	5	3	4	4	4	4	2	5	2	5	4	4	4	70-215
Ben Curtis	4	4	2	3	3	5	2	4	4	4	5	4	5	3	5	4	5	4	70-217
Ross Fisher	4	5	4	3	4	4	3	4	5	6	3	3	4	2	5	4	4	4	71-217
Anthony Kim	4	4	5	4	4	5	3	4	4	4	4	3	4	3	5	4	3	4	71-217
Alexander Noren	5	7	4	3	4	4	3	4	4	4	4	4	5	3	4	5	4	4	75-217
Henrik Stenson	5	4	4	3	4	4	3	4	3	4	4	3	4	3	4	6	4	4	70-218
Graeme Storm	4	4	3	3	4	5	4	4	4	4	4	4	4	4	5	4	4	4	72-218
Chris Wood*	5	5	4	4	3	5	3	4	4	5	4	3	4	3	5	4	4	4	73-218
Ian Poulter	4	4	4	4	4	5	3	4	4	4	4	4	4	3	6	4	6	4	75-218
Robert Allenby	5	4	5	3	4	5	3	4	4	5	4	4	4	3	6	4	4	5	76-218
Rocco Mediate	6	4	4	4	4	5	4	3	5	4	4	4	5	3	5	4	4	4	76-218

* Denotes amateur

son got into the bunker and his ball duly moved. However, The R&A's Rules Director, David Rickman, deemed that since it was known that it was not the player who had caused the ball to move there should be no penalty in this case. Ironically, exactly the same happened to the Swede later at the 17th.

It was a supremely difficult day for everyone, from players to rules officials to spectators. Only four players matched par and no one went under it.

The 70 of Ben Curtis included a moment of fortune when he holed out with a nine iron for an eagle at the third. He looked disgusted with the shot because he thought he had lost it to the right on the wind, but a kindly bounce intervened. But the 2003 Champion also played some fine golf, as validated by his playing partner Mickelson. Curtis, whose effort meant he stayed at seven over for the Championship, started the day tied for 38th place. When he holed out on the 18th he had moved up to a tie for 19th. At day's end he was tied for fifth, alongside Kim, Ross Fisher, and Alexander Noren.

Anthony Kim came in with 71, having eagle-3 at No 17.

Testing weather conditions did not deter the spectators, who numbered 201,500 for the week.

Graeme Storm was joint ninth after 72.

Ahead of him stood Wakefield, another to score 70, at five over; Choi, after a 75, and Harrington, with 72, at four over; and Norman at the head of affairs on two over after 72.

Aside from the Saturday afternoon storm at Muirfield in 2002 and the opening day at Royal Troon in 2004, there had not been a windier Open since Birkdale 10 years earlier. Then the Saturday was brutal as well. The 1998 scoring average was 77.5, compared to 75.8 this year, while back then 23 of the 81 players failed to break 80. This time nine players out of the 83 who had qualified for the weekend scored 80 or higher, including Justin Rose with 82 and David Duval with 83.

Phillip Archer, the 36 year-old from nearby Warrington playing in his first Open, was the first man out and returned not unhappily with 78. "You can't not enjoy playing in The Open," he said. Paul Casey needed the help of HRH The Duke of York in trying to find his ball in the rough at the 15th but to no avail. The prince was not surprised. He had lost a ball in the same spot only a week before. Davis Love III and Henrik Stenson both scored 70s before Curtis came in with the same mark, while Fisher and Kim, two talented newcomers from England and America playing together,

Steve Stricker had just two bogeys in his 71.

Ross Fisher was three under par on the last eight holes.

Third Round Scores	
Players Below Par	0
Players At Par	4
Players Above Par	79

Jim Furyk took 43 on the second nine, tumbling to 77.

Excerpts
FROM THE Press

"Simon Wakefield, an unknown 34 year-old Englishman who has never won an event on golf's European Tour, goes into the final day of The 137th Open at Royal Birkdale with the chance of becoming one of the Championship's most unlikely winners."

—Peter Higgs, *The Mail on Sunday*

"If there was anything clear and uncomplicated to emerge from the buffeting Royal Birkdale took, it was that despite all that wind the lowest front-nine score of the tournament so far was recorded. It came from Ben Curtis of the United States, who took the gusts in his stride as he scored a commendable 31 which included an eagle."

—Peter Corrigan, *The Independent on Sunday*

"And you thought golf would be boring without one Tiger Woods. What we have unfolding here on the wind-whipped dunes bordering the Irish Sea is a major as exciting, with even more twists and personality, than the one that just captivated us at Torrey Pines."

—Melanie Hauser, PGATOUR.com

"Anthony Kim caused a Birkdale traffic jam when 50mph winds blew his ball 15 yards off a green. The young sensation of American golf had to wait almost 45 minutes for the gales battering the exposed 10th green to die down before he could replace his ball to the original spot and finish the hole."

—Brian McSweeney, *Sunday Mail*

Simon Wakefield equalled the day's low round with 70, including 34 on the last nine.

Despite posting 75, KJ Choi was joint second on 214, two strokes off the lead.

both returned 71s to get a later tee-time for Sunday. Chris Wood, the amateur qualifier, had 73 to be eight over and took a significant lead over Thomas Sherreard in the race for the Silver Medal.

Wakefield had come to watch both the 1991 and 1998 Opens at Royal Birkdale but had never played the course before this week. The 34 year-old from Newcastle-under-Lyme had yet to win on the European Tour, but during the winter would travel just over an hour to north Wales and play links courses like Conwy to keep in practice. His 34 on the second nine matched the best of the day and included birdies at both the par-3s, the 12th and the 14th, where he chipped in from behind the green, and also at the 17th. "I may not sleep a lot tonight," he said. "Obviously, this is very unfamiliar territory for me."

Wakefield's uncle is Bob Taylor, the former England wicketkeeper —

Low Scores

Low First Nine	
Ben Curtis	31
Low Second Nine	
Anthony Kim	34
Simon Wakefield	34
Low Round	
Davis Love III	70
Henrik Stenson	70
Ben Curtis	70
Simon Wakefield	70

Even with 76, Rocco Mediate retained a top-10 position.

and he gets asked about him in every interview. "I don't see him very often, but he sends me a text every now and then." There would be one now. Taylor played in one of the most famous Test matches ever, when England, having been quoted at odds of 500-1 such was their parlous position in the match, produced an amazing recovery to beat Australia at Headingley in 1981. Norman's odds at the start of this Open were also 500-1, but by the end of the third round they were down to 4-1.

After the pairing of Wakefield and Garcia (74), the last 11 twoballs produced only two scores under 75 (Norman and Harrington) and four in the 80s. The most surprising was perhaps that of McDowell, who had headed out as if it was a "nice, sunny, breezy day" at Portrush but came back 10 strokes worse off. With an outward 34, including birdies at the eighth and the ninth, Jim Furyk briefly tied for the lead with Choi and Harrington before a double bogey at the

Padraig Harrington offset a double bogey and four bogeys with four birdies.

Amateurs Thrive Again On Birkdale Links

Royal Birkdale's reputation for igniting the careers of aspiring amateur golfers, which was stoked in 1998 when Justin Rose tied for fourth, was enhanced during The Open after Chris Wood, the young Englishman, signed for 73 in the third round and put himself in position to claim the Silver Medal for leading amateur.

While Wood went on to make another leap in the Championship after posting 72 for 10-over 290 on Sunday — a score which moved him up to a share of fifth place — his dogged display in carding 73 on Saturday in high winds ensured the 20 year-old from Bristol improved his position with each passing day.

He was tied for 52nd on Thursday after opening with 75, tied for 22nd on Friday after 70, and tied for ninth on Saturday after scoring three over par in spite of starting his round with successive bogeys. "I finished well with three 4s," he recalled. "That was my target for the closing stretch — finish one under and try to get in on 73. It was a battle and I battled all the way round."

In addition to Wood, amateur Thomas Sherreard, another 20 year-old from Leicester, also advanced to the weekend with his 69 on Friday and earned a share of 19th place in the final standings. Both Wood and Sherreard were making their Open debuts.

A tall, slim fellow with a narrow waist, Wood relished his first appearance at an Open with a combination of stalwart golf and engaging modesty. On Sunday he would play with Ian Poulter and pretty much hold his own in the company of one of golf's most flamboyant characters.

By finishing in the top five at Birkdale, Wood is exempt to tee up in The Open at Turnberry in July of 2009, irrespective of his amateur or professional status. Although his initial reaction to playing so well in Southport was to take a bit of time to consider his future and stay in the amateur ranks until after the 2009 Walker Cup in America, Wood didn't disguise his ambition.

"I'm keen to turn pro," Wood said. "That's why you put in all the hours, to contend in championships like The Open. Obviously, I'd like to contend a little bit more in the years to come."

He paid tribute to family and friends for their support, as well as the English Golf Union, who sent him to play in Australia, Argentina, Mexico, and Russia. "The standard of amateur golf is so high that many of the guys who turned pro this year or last are already doing well after coming straight out of the England team," Wood said.

Once a promising centre-forward who joined the football academy at Bristol City before suffering a knee injury which persuaded him to concentrate on golf, Wood was the EGU's Order of Merit winner in 2007.

Had he already been a member of the professional ranks, Wood would have taken home a cheque for around £168,500 for his performance at Royal Birkdale. Instead, he'll retain a treasure trove of memories.

With his father, Richard, who plays off a 4 handicap, on the bag, and a 60-strong contingent of relatives, friends, and members from Long Ashton in Bristol cheering him on, Wood relished a sterling performance and "the best week of my life."

—Mike Aitken

After his 5-7 start, Alexander Noren played well for 75 to tie for fifth place.

10th set up an inward 43. Rocco Mediate had 76 and Camilo Villegas, 79, but Ian Poulter, pretty in pink, snuck round in 75 to be lurking at eight over despite dropping shots at the par-5 15th and 17th holes.

When Choi, after five pars, drove into a pot bunker at the sixth and took a double bogey, no one was under par and no one would be again this week. Problems were mounting everywhere. "I would put it in the top three hardest rounds I've ever played under the conditions," Norman said. "I've played under tougher weather conditions, but in the third round of a major championship on the Royal Birkdale golf course, it was just brutal today."

Choi was marvelling at Norman's shot-making

Posting 73 in the high winds helped Chris Wood to the Silver Medal.

ability. "He is a very imaginative player," said the Korean, "more imaginative than me." Norman was banking on all his experience and giving a master class in feeling his way round the course. At the fifth hole he hit a five iron onto the green from only 120 yards. "The yardage was mentioned to me, but I didn't even pay attention to it," Norman explained. "I already saw the shot that I knew I had to play to get the ball close to the hole." Elsewhere there was a seven iron from 104 yards, and at the 17th he found the green with a second shot of 209 yards played with a six iron that started out over the grandstand to the left of the green.

But the problems only got worse once a player was on the green. Without the rain of the opening two days to slow the surface, putting was becoming a ticklish endeavour. "I think those were the toughest

"They were right when they said it wouldn't be the same without Tiger Woods. It's been even better. A fading legend who refuses to see sense, a defending Champion clinging for dear life to the Claret Jug, and a leading Englishman who isn't even the most famous sportsman in his family: This 137th Open Championship has had just about everything, and it isn't finished yet."

—Paul Forsyth, *The Sunday Times*

"On the third day of its Championship, Birkdale showed not a jot of mercy. Nobody broke par on a brutal day of gusting wind, but the show laid on by two players who could not be of more contrasting appearance outdid even the weather. And when they were joined by the defending Champion, it all added up to a wonderful piece of sporting theatre."

—Eddie Butler, *The Observer*

"Phil Mickelson's cap was blown to the four winds. Lee Westwood said he couldn't take the pressure, and local boy Nick Dougherty's dream of singing, 'You'll Never Walk Alone' to the horde of Liverpool fans will have to wait a few more years. The third round of The Open at Royal Birkdale was a scene of majestic carnage as an avenging wind whipped in off the Irish Sea and blew the field apart."

—Mark Reason, *The Sunday Telegraph*

Playing the last eight holes in two under, Norman led for the eighth time entering the final round of a major championship.

conditions to putt in I've ever experienced," said Harrington. "There was no sense of preparation over any putt. By the time you got over it, you still hadn't got any clarity in the line. You still hadn't got any clarity in how hard you were going to hit it, because you weren't sure what the wind was going to do to it."

Harrington went to the turn in 34, holing a pitch from the rough at the fifth for a birdie and hitting a five iron to six feet at the seventh for another. The crowd, containing no few Irishmen, were now roaring him on, eager to help if he ever went off line and wincing in sympathy over the wrist if he had to play out of the rough. When Choi bogeyed the eighth, Harrington found himself tied for the lead. Not that he knew. "I never saw a leaderboard," he said. "I kept my head down and didn't look once. I had no idea how the leaders were doing. I knew everyone would find it tough."

He knew from the adventures of his playing partner, Duval, who was out in 44 without playing particularly badly. But suddenly Harrington's round found trouble. He three-putted at the 11th and then

Round of the Day

**OFFICIAL SCORECARD
THE OPEN CHAMPIONSHIP 2008
Royal Birkdale**

Greg NORMAN
Game 42
Saturday 19 July at 2:40 pm

FOR R&A USE ONLY 42.1

36 HOLE TOTAL __140__
THIS ROUND __72__
54 HOLE TOTAL __212__

ROUND 3
54 HOLE TOTAL
212

VERIFIED _____

ROUND 3

Hole	1	2	3	4	5	6	7	8	9	Out	10	11	12	13	14	15	16	17	18	In	Total
Yards	450	421	451	201	346	499	178	457	414	3417	408	436	184	499	201	544	439	572	473	3756	7173
Par	4	4	4	3	4	4	3	4	4	34	4	4	3	4	3	5	4	5	4	36	70
Score	5	4	5	3	4	5	3	3	4	36	6	4	3	4	2	5	4	4	4	36	72

Signature of Marker

Signature of Competitor   Greg Norman

Greg Norman spared no words in expressing his pride in his two-over-par 72 score in the 40-50mph wind gusts of the third day that left him with a two-stroke lead in The Open Championship.

"I would put it in the top three hardest rounds I've ever played under the conditions," Norman said. "I've played under tougher weather conditions, but under the circumstances, the third round of a major championship on the Royal Birkdale golf course, it was just brutal today....

"It was so hard to start the ball 60 or 80 yards right or left of your target line. The wind was so heavy and so strong, like I have never seen it. KJ (Choi, his mate in the final pairing) and I were talking about it. I've never seen the ball react like it did once it hit its apex. Once it got above the sand dune line, it was at the mercy of the elements. It was incredible to watch, actu-

ally, to see the golf ball react like it was reacting."

Norman was three over par on the day after dropping shots on the first, third, and sixth holes, but got one back with a 10-foot putt on the par-4 eighth. He took 6 for double bogey on the 10th, but did not let another stroke slip away. He struck a six iron to 12 feet for birdie on the par-3 14th and took two putts from 25 feet on the par-5 17th for another birdie.

caught a gust at the short 12th and went over the green. It was a nasty spot in the rough on a bank, but he got it onto the green and then three-putted for a double-bogey 5.

Yet once more, Harrington failed to be distracted by a couple of poor holes. He finished with two birdies at the 15th and 17th and only dropped one more shot at the 16th, after finding rough off the tee and a greenside bunker. Down in two from the back of the 18th and he was the first to the clubhouse at four over. He seemed to be ready for more of the same the next day. "I'd look forward to that challenge," he said. "If it was high winds it would probably give me my best chance of winning."

The 36 year-old had come from six strokes behind Garcia at Carnoustie, but now, with Choi unable to beat his score, he would be going out on Sunday in the final pairing with Norman.

"There is no comparison to last year," Harrington said. "Last year I went out in the last round under no particular stress, just go

Ben Curtis

Dreams Of Another Open Title

It was in May, at the Wachovia Championship in North Carolina, that Ben Curtis gave a strong indication that he was back where he had been in that July week in 2003 when he came from nowhere to win The Open at Royal St George's. In handing in rounds of 69, 71, 72, and 65 over the Quail Hollow course, he had avoided the one high round which had been "a killer" in so many of his other outings in 2008. He placed second by five shots to Anthony Kim.

Back in February, for example, Curtis had a third-round 76 at the Northern Trust Open in Los Angeles, which had him sliding into a tie for 62nd place. Later, in that same month, he opened with rounds of 73, 71, and 66 in the Honda Classic in Florida, before amassing a closing 78 that placed him in a tie for 65th.

When it came to Royal Birkdale, Curtis was operating under the radar — he had opening rounds of 78 and 69 — until it came to the third hole of his third round.

Taking into account the fact that he was standing with the ball a little below his feet, he opted for a nine iron for the 165 yards he had to the flag. He felt he had heeled it and waited for the greenside groan which would accompany a shot being snapped up by the right-hand bunker. Instead, he heard a crescendo of applause before finally everyone went crazy as the ball dropped for 2, an eagle.

He followed up with a birdie at the 346-yard fifth, where he hit a six iron to 25 feet, before pinning down another 2 at the 178-yard seventh, where he shaped a four iron to six feet. Out in 31 in conditions which, as Curtis himself described as "about as tough as you can play in," he covered the second nine in 39 for the 70 which left him on 217 — seven over par and five off the lead. Coming home, as he saw it, had been all about "hanging on for dear life."

Curtis did not mind admitting that his big dream was to win a second Open. "If I had a choice of majors for my second, this would be it," he maintained.

Though he had not won on the PGA Tour since 2004, he had notched a handful of top-five finishes and proved to himself that there were weeks when he was playing well enough to have the beating of the rest. His problem, he thought, was that his expectations were too high.

He added that, overall, he believed himself to be a far better player than he had been in 2003. Then, though, he made everyone laugh with the very pertinent suggestion that everybody else in the field was probably better than he was five years ago.

—Lewine Mair

Narrowly avoiding 80, Camilo Villegas saved par on No 18 for his 79.

"With so much baggage behind him in the majors, Greg Norman did all he could not to look too far ahead. He is 18 holes from becoming golf's oldest major champion, but he wouldn't bite when asked what it would feel like to win. 'Ask me that question tomorrow night if it happens, OK?' he said."

—Doug Ferguson,
The Associated Press

"This must be what they mean by royal pain. Winds of almost historic magnitude ... played havoc with the third round of The 137th Open Championship, but when the dust settled, things looked pretty much as they started."

—Dave Perkins, *Toronto Star*

"On a day Lahinch patrons would have described as ideal for ground hurling, Padraig Harrington maintained the defence of his Open title in punishing, gale-force winds at Royal Birkdale. The reigning Champion shot a marvellous 72 for a share of second place, but Graeme McDowell, the other Irish survivor, had a wretched 6-5-6 finish to plummet out of contention after 80."

—Dermot Gilleece,
Sunday Independent

"If Greg Norman was told that every Irish man, woman, and child who'll be watching the final round of The Open Championship will be hoping he won't go down as the oldest major winner in history, he'd probably laugh."

—Mark Jones, *Sunday Tribune*

out and anything can happen. Tomorrow I'd love to have the same attitude, but obviously it's going to be a tighter day. Last year I was the only person I had to focus on because I needed to go forward to have a chance to win. Tomorrow, you'll be watching what's going on and you're not sure whether having a great day or a steady day will be good enough. I'll have to stay patient and see if I've got the experience to manage to do it."

As for the leader, Harrington said: "He is as fit a 53 year-old as there is, and when he puts his mind to it, he can certainly play. He hasn't lost any of his ability. I don't think anybody should expect anything but good play from him tomorrow."

Norman still had to finish off today. He had bogeyed three of the first six holes but got one back at the eighth and was tied for the lead with Choi. After a long wait on the 10th tee, due to all the backups, both men took 6s to start the second nine. But from then on Norman did not miss a shot. At the 13th, Choi rolled in a 25-footer from just outside Norman for a birdie, but the Korean dropped one at the 15th to fall back alongside Harrington at four over.

Round Three Hole Summary

HOLE	PAR	YARDS	EAGLES	BIRDIES	PARS	BOGEYS	D.BOGEYS	HIGHER	RANK	AVERAGE
1	4	450	0	1	40	31	8	3	2	4.663
2	4	421	0	1	52	26	3	1	6	4.410
3	4	451	1	7	52	21	2	0	14	4.193
4	3	201	0	2	44	34	2	1	5	3.470
5	4	346	0	8	55	17	3	0	15	4.181
6	4	499	0	1	26	45	11	0	1	4.795
7	3	178	0	8	46	27	2	0	9	3.277
8	4	457	0	10	56	15	1	1	17	4.120
9	4	414	0	6	59	17	1	0	16	4.157
OUT	**34**	**3417**	**1**	**44**	**430**	**233**	**33**	**6**		**37.266**
10	4	408	0	1	47	21	11	3	3	4.614
11	4	436	0	5	60	15	1	2	11	4.229
12	3	184	0	2	41	34	4	2	4	3.566
13	4	499	0	5	50	22	4	2	7	4.373
14	3	201	0	7	51	20	5	0	10	3.277
15	5	544	0	10	49	21	3	0	13	5.205
16	4	439	0	9	52	17	5	0	12	4.217
17	5	572	2	36	36	7	1	1	18	4.675
18	4	473	0	3	53	24	2	1	8	4.337
IN	**36**	**3756**	**2**	**78**	**439**	**181**	**36**	**11**		**38.493**
TOTAL	**70**	**7173**	**3**	**122**	**869**	**414**	**69**	**17**		**75.759**

Henrik Stenson fell to joint ninth with double-bogey 6 on No 16.

Now the final pairing was picking up an enormous gallery and the atmosphere was terrific. Norman responded by hitting a six iron to 12 feet at the short 14th and holing the putt to get to three over. He arrived on the 17th tee with the lead and might have ended the day with a commanding advantage. At the par-5 his approach climbed the ridge but not with quite enough momentum and the ball rolled down to the lower tier. Nevertheless, his eagle try was right on line and only just missed. The birdie put him at two over.

Up the last and the ovation was thundering again. But he had pushed his approach, only for this to produce the thrilling finale of almost holing his chip. The ball caught the lip but finished a couple of inches away. Yet once again Norman led a major with a round to play. The first four times came in 1986, when he went on to win The Open at Turnberry but also suffered the first of many last-day

Davis Love III returned 70, advancing to a tie for 15th.

Retief Goosen, with 73, was also joint 15th on nine over par.

nightmares when Jack Nicklaus, at the age of 46, swooped to take away the green jacket at the Masters. The last time Norman led after 54 had been in 1996, also at Augusta, when a six-stroke advantage over Nick Faldo had not proved enough.

Norman, ranked No 646 in the world following his limited appearances, admitted that less than two months before, when he elected to play in his first Open for three years, had someone told him he would be leading at this stage his reaction would have been a bewildered: "Oh, really?"

"I am going to keep the same mindset," he said. "Obviously, I played well enough to put myself in this position. That comes from a good, safe, happy

Ian Poulter took bogey-6 on the two par-5 holes.

"

"Am I allowed to say bloody tough? Yes? Bloody tough then. The toughest I've played in was when I won the Australian Open in 2005, but this one took the cake."

—**Robert Allenby**

"I will definitely bring more bad weather gear (in the future) and learn my wind shots."

—**Anthony Kim**

"Just thoroughly enjoying the Open experience. The crowd out there are absolutely crazy. The reception all the way round the course for not only myself but Anthony (Kim) was absolutely tremendous."

—**Ross Fisher**

"This is my first Open and it's just been a great experience."

—**Chris Wood**

"So many shots, so many putts were hit with the ball wobbling. It was close to calling it off for a while."

—**Sergio Garcia**

"I am extremely disappointed with my score (83). I can assure you very few people hit the ball better than I did today."

—**David Duval**

"

Camilo Villegas, Greg Norman, and Rocco Mediate wait out a delay.

Robert Allenby stayed in the top 10.

Sergio Garcia had 74 to be joint 15th.

mind in a lot of ways. I am very content, and now I have the lead it's going to be tough again tomorrow, but I'm going out with the same mindset.

"Physically, I'm not tired. Mentally, I'm not tired, although you had to work a little bit harder even over those putts a foot to 18 inches long. I'll be honest, I walked to the first tee nervous today. It was a good indictor for me that I was as nervous as I felt. I hadn't felt that way for 10 years, maybe longer. I was excited about being there. I wanted to be there. I hope to feel the same way tomorrow and I hope I can keep it going."

Norman Defies The Gales

'I would put it in the top three hardest rounds I've ever played'

By Alistair Tait

The Open has thrown up some intriguing story lines over the years, but it's hard to imagine a more fascinating tale than that of Gregory John Norman in 2008.

At least 10 years past his prime, and playing only part-time golf, Greg Norman did the unthinkable for the first two days of The 137th Open Championship: He stayed in the hunt. Two level-par rounds of 70 put him just one shot off KJ Choi's lead heading into the weekend. Everyone at Royal Birkdale feared the worst on Saturday. Surely the Great White Shark couldn't continue the dream.

Could he?

Norman answered that question emphatically with a round of 72 in the harsh conditions that continued to plague the Southport links. That score produced the unlikeliest of third-round stories. Norman sat atop the heap in the game's premier event with one round to go.

"I would put it in the top three hardest rounds I've ever played," Norman said after taming the 35-40mph winds with one of the best scores of the day. "It was just brutal today."

The two-time Open Champion bogeyed three of the first six holes, made a double bogey at the 10th, but managed to rescue his round with birdies at the eighth, 14th, and 17th holes. When the sun finally set on the third day, he held a two-shot lead on the field.

The conditions were so harsh that Norman ended up ignoring his yardage book for much of the round. He called in all his experience of 26 years playing in The Open Championship to produce the type of shots needed in the tough links conditions.

"I think only the individuals who have been there before know what to do. It's like seeing shots I hit today from 120 yards with a five iron. I didn't even pay attention to the yardage. I knew that was the shot to get the ball close to the hole. I did that three, four, maybe five times today."

That the Australian could return such a score on a day when there were nine scores in the 80s defied all logic. Norman hadn't competed in an Open Championship since 2005 at St Andrews. He hadn't been close to adding to his Open victories in 1986 and 1993 since finishing sixth at Carnoustie nine years previously.

"I walked to the first tee nervous today. It was a good indicator for me. I hadn't felt that way probably for 10 years, maybe even longer. I was excited about being there. I wanted to be there."

At one point earlier in the year Norman wasn't even considering playing at Birkdale. He only committed two months before to get ready for the Senior Open at Royal Troon the following week, and the US Senior Open the week after.

All week Norman has been telling everyone that he worked harder on his tennis than his golf. New wife Chris Evert was responsible for that. The couple married on June 29. In the months leading up to Birkdale,

Norman played tennis about three times a week, calling himself an 18-20 handicap at that other ball game.

Evert wasn't only responsible for helping Norman maintain his athletic shape, but for giving him new peace of mind following his divorce. "I came in here with a good attitude and a fresh approach to life in general, and it's really showed through in my game," Norman said.

While everyone was rubbing the disbelief out of their eyes to make sure what they were seeing was actually happening, Norman was the least surprised man in town.

"I think it's a great indicator for every player out there, whether you're just coming on the tour for the first year or you're turning 40 or in your 50s. The game of golf is there to be played. If you go in there with the right attitude and keep yourself physically fit, you can put yourself in that position no matter what.

"If I'm a young kid, looking now and seeing a guy at 53 years old leading the Open and I'm only 18, I'm going to say, boy, I've got a lot of years left in my career."

Norman's position leading the tournament backed up a prediction he made before the tournament began: "I made the comment at the start of the week that a dark horse could have a chance around here because of the conditions. Royal Birkdale doesn't suit anybody, but suits everybody."

Whether he meant a Great White Shark could turn into a huge dark horse was debatable. Either way it was eerily prophetic.

It was the stuff of fairytales. In fact, this tale was so fairy-like that even Nick Faldo got excited.

Faldo approached Norman immediately after his third round and put his arms around him.

"What you are doing is awesome," Faldo told Norman. "I'm rooting for you."

So it seemed was almost everyone else at Royal Birkdale.

Fourth Round

Champion Another Year

By Andy Farrell

Harrington defends his title and becomes Royal Birkdale's first European winner.

As on any Sunday in golf, all but one man's dreams were shattered by the end of The 137th Open Championship. Walking down the 18th fairway, Padraig Harrington turned to Greg Norman and said: "I'm sorry it isn't your story that is being told this evening." Some stories are destined to remain fairytales and among them at Royal Birkdale were the thought that a 53 year-old former Champion could grab one last heroic slice of glory or a 20 year-old amateur could claim the most prized possession in golf. Even a gutsy finish from a talented Englishman was not good enough if facts are to be faced. No, the best yarns are always from Ireland.

Norman gave the final round a romantic appeal, Chris Wood provided the innocence of youth, and Ian Poulter, trousered in pink but with more granite than pastel in his game, an injection of spirited defiance. But nothing could stop Harrington's

Padraig Harrington shared his delight with son Patrick.

brilliant yet serene charge to retain his title. Having mentally conquered the twin demons of the teasing conditions and his own wandering mind, the Irishman's physical execution over a last nine of 32, the lowest of the day, was flawless. Birkdale had its first European winner, the supreme course yielding a supreme Champion.

Three approach shots of stunning quality sealed a four-stroke victory over Poulter after a closing 69 gave him a total of 283, three over par. The first of these came at the 13th hole, where a birdie changed the complexion of his, and everyone else's, day; the second at the 17th, setting up the victorious eagle; the third at the last for a Champion's finale. Harrington was then soon ushered forward to collect the Claret Jug once more, the Champion golfer of another year.

"I'm holding on to this," he told the gallery at the 18th as he cradled the trophy in his arms. "I had a great year as Open Champion, so much so that I didn't want to give it back." Giving the trophy back to The R&A at the start of the week had been hard, but even that worked out well in the end. "It's a little shinier than I remember,"

4

Fourth Round Leaders

HOLE	1	2	3	4	5	6	7	8	9	10	11	12	13	14	15	16	17	18	TOTAL
PAR	4	4	4	3	4	4	3	4	4	4	4	3	4	3	5	4	5	4	
Padraig Harrington	4	4	4	3	4	4	4	5	5	4	4	3	3	3	4	4	3	4	69-283
Ian Poulter	5	4	5	3	4	4	3	4	3	4	3	3	4	3	5	3	5	4	69-287
Henrik Stenson	5	4	4	3	4	5	3	4	3	4	4	3	4	4	4	4	4	5	71-289
Greg Norman	5	5	5	3	4	5	3	4	4	5	4	4	5	3	4	4	5	5	77-289
Jim Furyk	5	5	4	3	4	4	3	4	4	4	4	3	4	3	4	4	5	4	71-290
Chris Wood*	4	4	5	3	4	4	2	4	3	4	5	4	5	3	5	4	4	5	72-290
David Howell	4	4	5	3	3	4	2	4	4	4	3	4	4	3	4	4	3	5	67-292
Robert Karlsson	3	4	4	3	4	4	3	4	4	5	3	3	4	3	5	5	4	4	69-292
Ernie Els	4	4	4	2	4	4	3	4	4	5	4	3	4	3	4	4	5	4	69-292
Paul Casey	4	4	4	4	4	4	3	4	4	5	5	3	4	3	3	4	4	4	70-292
Stephen Ames	4	5	5	3	3	4	3	3	4	5	4	3	4	3	5	4	5	4	71-292
Steve Stricker	4	4	4	3	5	5	4	4	4	4	4	3	4	3	5	4	5	4	73-292
Robert Allenby	3	5	4	3	4	7	3	4	4	5	4	3	5	3	6	4	3	4	74-292
Anthony Kim	4	4	4	3	4	5	3	4	4	4	5	3	4	3	5	5	6	5	75-292
Ben Curtis	5	3	5	3	4	4	3	5	4	4	4	4	5	3	4	4	6	5	75-292

* Denotes amateur

David Howell's 67 was low round of the day.

he said. "They obviously cleaned it up nicely. I'm looking forward to getting it back in its rightful spot on the breakfast table." It would no longer be a receptacle for ladybirds, son Patrick now keener on snails and "other more gruesome creatures," the father reported.

Harrington added: "I never put last year down as an isolated event. I felt I was going to win another one, but it's come round quicker than I thought. Never at any stage, or if I did for a second or two I stopped myself, did I think about what it means to win a second Open. Obviously winning a major puts you in a special club. Winning two of them puts you in a new club altogether."

He was eager to discover who else had won consecutive Opens. Told the names of Woods, Watson, Trevino, Palmer, Thomson, Locke, and Jones, Harrington replied: "That's very good company." It was the first time since James Braid in 1906 that a European golfer had defended the title. It was also the first time for almost 80 years that consecutive Champions had won back-to-back:

Bobby Jones (1926-27) and Walter Hagen (1928-29) linking with Tiger Woods (2005-06) and Harrington.

Many were the differences with Carnoustie from a year earlier. His wins were with and without Tiger; achieved by overcoming a six-stroke deficit and by going out in the final pairing; by stumbling into a playoff and by racing away from the field; by the fortune of someone else's misfortune (when Sergio Garcia missed his putt to win) and by removing luck from the equation all together. "There is a different satisfaction this year," Harrington said. "Last year was a great high, it was a great thrill, and it was exciting and unexpected, and I was on top of the world when I won.

"This year is more satisfying. I feel more accomplished. It was the first time I was in the last group of a major on a Sunday. It's a different pressure, it's a different stress, and to shoot under par and come through all that and win by a few shots will give me a lot more confidence."

Both the week's weather and the wrist injury that curtailed his practice earlier in the week turned out to be beneficial. "They say beware the injured golfer, but I think my case was different to Tiger's at the US Open. He was obviously injured, but my injury did not impair me at all on the golf course. I didn't think

Sunday Weather

Sunny spells, a few blustery showers early on, dry and mainly clear in afternoon. Winds NW 20-25mph, gusts 30-35mph.

Here at No 6, Greg Norman stumbled with four bogeys in his first six holes.

Round Four Hole Summary

HOLE	PAR	YARDS	EAGLES	BIRDIES	PARS	BOGEYS	D.BOGEYS	HIGHER	RANK	AVERAGE
1	4	450	0	3	39	35	6	0	2	4.530
2	4	421	0	11	55	14	2	1	12	4.120
3	4	451	0	5	52	25	1	0	7	4.265
4	3	201	0	4	49	28	2	0	5	3.337
5	4	346	0	10	59	12	2	0	15	4.072
6	4	499	0	3	31	40	7	2	1	4.687
7	3	178	0	8	54	21	0	0	10	3.157
8	4	457	0	9	56	17	1	0	13	4.120
9	4	414	0	14	55	12	0	2	16	4.048
OUT	**34**	**3417**	**0**	**67**	**450**	**204**	**21**	**5**		**36.336**
10	4	408	0	1	46	31	4	1	4	4.494
11	4	436	0	10	52	15	3	3	8	4.253
12	3	184	0	6	59	18	0	0	11	3.145
13	4	499	0	2	56	20	5	0	6	4.337
14	3	201	0	2	62	18	1	0	9	3.217
15	5	544	1	24	47	8	3	0	18	4.855
16	4	439	0	6	62	15	0	0	14	4.108
17	5	572	4	26	35	14	3	1	17	4.867
18	4	473	0	3	45	28	5	2	3	4.518
IN	**36**	**3756**	**5**	**80**	**464**	**167**	**24**	**7**		**37.794**
TOTAL	**70**	**7173**	**5**	**147**	**914**	**371**	**45**	**12**		**74.130**

A look behind the scenes at the new 18th hole leaderboards, replicas of the originals.

about it once today. But what it did do was keep me away from practising earlier in the week and pushed everything about coming back to defend to the back of my mind. And there's no question the weather forced me to play one shot at a time and stay with my own game. I do have a wandering mind and have struggled sometimes when I've been in the lead. The weather kept me focused on what I had to do."

Once again the wind was blowing, not quite as hard as on Saturday, or as awkwardly gusting, but a good 30mph-plus force of nature. Good for the Tall Ships down in Liverpool Docks, but only adding to the challenge of Birkdale. "It's a great course," said Justin Rose, the 1998 hero. "I don't know why it creates so much drama, but it does." The same tee changes from the third round were retained, while the 10th tee was also moved forward 27 yards.

After starting with two bogeys, Jim Furyk posted 71.

Also, the hole locations took into account, where possible, the slopes counteracting the wind rather than exacerbating them. Some early morning rain helped the earlier starters, and David Howell returned the day's best score of 67 to set an early clubhouse target of 12 over par.

Having started the day tied for 64th, Howell finished tied for seventh place and was joined by Ernie Els, whose 69 meant he was the only player other than Harrington to have two rounds under par, and Paul Casey who, on a hole where he lost a ball the day before, holed an outrageous pitch from the rough for an eagle. Ben Curtis and Anthony Kim were among those who would fall back 12 over after rounds of 75, but the mark was not bettered for hours and hours until Jim Furyk posted 10 over. The American started with two bogeys, but then added 15 pars and a birdie in his 71.

By the time Norman and Harrington got to the first tee, the danger of the opening holes was obvious. In the group in front KJ Choi and Simon Wakefield both bogeyed the first. Choi completely lost his rhythm on the short putts in the wind over the weekend and would be out in 40. He had 8 at the last after sending one drive out of bounds and then taking an unplayable with the next and closed with 79. As did Wakefield, despite remaining within one of the lead

Henrik Stenson (above) had 71 to advance from ninth to tie for third. Robert Allenby (right) was in the top 10 all week and tied for seventh. Simon Wakefield (far right) returned 79, tumbling from fourth to a tie for 19th.

KJ Choi posted 79, having an outward 40 and finishing with a quadruple-bogey 8.

with a birdie at the fifth. But shots dribbled away at the next two holes and the slide was on. Sadly, he too suffered an 8, his coming at the 17th after a lost drive and then going out of bounds with the second shot with his second ball.

How different would the day's result have been if events at the first in the final pairing had gone the other way? Harrington came up way short with his second shot from the right semi-rough, but then Norman's four-iron approach caught a greenside bunker. Harrington pitched from 50 yards to six inches for a tap-in par. Norman, however, could not get close out of the bunker, and the bogey cut his overnight advantage of two strokes in half.

On the second tee Harrington removed his sweater. There were times later he admitted to being cold, but having made the switch there was no way it was going back on. He two-putted the second and holed a good par-saver at the third. In contrast Norman could not find the greens or save his par and opened with three bogeys to give Harrington the lead. On the Irishman went making his pars, having found the pace of the greens despite the tricky conditions.

Anthony Kim was in the top five until finishing 5-6-5.

His 69 pushed Robert Karlsson from 48th to a tie for seventh.

Fourth Round Scores	
Players Below Par	6
Players At Par	2
Players Above Par	75

His superb touch helped with long two-putts at the fifth and the sixth, while Norman dropped another shot at the latter.

Up ahead, the only player making a move was Wood, one of the few among the leaders to be out under par. He made 2 at the seventh and then hit his nine-iron approach to the ninth to three feet for a second birdie. Suddenly the gallery of 40,000, making the total for the week a superb 201,500 given the weather, was getting excited, and with reason. Although he never got closer than within three of the lead, Wood was up to tied third.

Harrington's thought for the day was to commit to every shot. "You had to accept good shots might not get good results, so you had to focus on being committed to what you were doing rather than get too results-orientated," he said. "The only time I didn't do that was at the seventh." He missed the green at the short hole and dropped his first stroke. So it wouldn't be a Faldoesque 18-par charge to victory. When he bogeyed the next two holes he wasn't even leading

There's More To Poulter Than His Trousers

At the start of the fourth round, Ian Poulter was six shots behind Greg Norman. He was in a position to pounce but, at least early on, people were focussing more on his peachy-coloured trousers than his play.

Poulter may not know how he is going to score on a given day, but he knows precisely what he is going to wear. A very real part of his pre-tournament preparation includes having each outfit at the ready. He checks on whether the crease in the relevant trousers is 100 percent the night before and, if it is not, he will administer a final pressing.

Two bogeys in the first three holes of his fourth round — "Not the best of starts," Poulter said — did not change people's focus. However, by the time he rolled home a birdie putt to be out in a 35, everyone was taking rather more of an interest in his golf.

It was as Norman and Harrington were struggling in mid-round that Poulter began to move up the leaderboard. He made another birdie on the 11th and then notched an even better one at the 16th where he holed from 18 feet.

Others acknowledge their birdies with a smile, but not Poulter. When this latest putt dropped after loitering on the lip, he let out a scream, punched the air several times, and fairly bristled with determination. At that, he was tied with Harrington who was five groups behind him.

Poulter needed to birdie the par-5 17th if he was going to take things further. Instead, he reached the green in two shots, only to take three putts. That was a bitter disappointment, but in a move which showed the steel of the player, he holed out at the last to secure a par and 69.

After he had signed his card, Poulter wisely desisted from talking to TV and the media. Instead, he headed for the practice ground to prepare for a possible playoff. He was standing in the practice ground manager's cabin as Harrington hit his second to 17, and when he saw the ball pull up no more than three feet or so away from the flag, he headed back to base. "Padraig could have found trouble with that one, but he hit the perfect shot," he said.

If, at that point, he was still kicking himself for the way he played the 17th, such feelings were never going to last for long. At 32, he had finally proved himself. Everyone — including Tiger Woods — had laughed, good-naturedly, when Poulter said earlier in the year that if he could only play to his potential, there would be only him and Tiger. Now, in the context of a major, he had demonstrated to all and sundry that he was every inch the good golfer he has always believed himself to be.

As one person after another congratulated him, so Poulter focussed more and more on the best aspects of his afternoon and his Open week.

"I don't think I've enjoyed a week as much as I have enjoyed this week," Poulter said. "It's on home soil, the crowd has been absolutely awesome, they've been driving me on. The chants have been awesome out on the golf course. To start holing putts around the back nine, to hear everybody screaming and shouting and driving you on is a massive adrenaline rush. It's a massive boost.

"You know, I've done my best, and it hasn't been quite good enough. But I'll be back for lots more of this. It's a nice roller coaster ride."

—Lewine Mair

'I thought right then I had a good chance to win,' said Ian Poulter of the 16th hole and his 18-foot birdie.

Missing the green at No 7, Harrington took the first of three successive bogeys and fell behind Norman.

any more. He three-putted the eighth green and did not get up and down from right of the ninth green. With Norman making three pars, to be out in 38 to Harrington's 37, the Australian was back in the lead by one.

As champions do, both Harrington and Norman realised a crucial moment had arrived at the 10th. Norman was in trouble, struggling to save par, but when Harrington's birdie attempt ran on four feet past the hole, so too was the Irishman. On one of the most exposed greens on the course, he now faced a tricky return. Without the wind he would have hit it "left lip." With the wind, he had to hit it "right half." He holed it, but like every putt out there he had to watch it all the way into the hole. "That putt really settled him down," Norman observed.

Wood's Cinderella moment came to an end with three bogeys in a row from the 11th, including at the 12th where he left an awkward bunker shot in the sand. But he went on to finish tied for fifth, the best result by an amateur in The Open since Rose's fourth-place tie at Birkdale 10 years earlier. "It's been the week of my life," Wood

Round of the **Day**

Padraig HARRINGTON
Game 42
Sunday 20 July at 2:20 pm

FOR R&A USE ONLY 42.1
54 HOLE TOTAL   214
THIS ROUND   69
72 HOLE TOTAL   283

ROUND 4
72 HOLE TOTAL
283

VERIFIED   CTB

ROUND 4

Hole	1	2	3	4	5	6	7	8	9	Out
Yards	450	421	451	201	346	499	178	457	414	3417
Par	4	4	4	3	4	4	3	4	4	34
Score	4	4	4	3	4	4	5	5		37

10	11	12	13	14	15	16	17	18	In	Total
408	436	184	499	201	544	439	572	473	3756	7173
4	4	3	4	3	5	4	5	4	36	70
4	4	3	3	3	4	4	3	4	32	69

Signature
of Marker

Signature of
Competitor   Padraig Harrington

"In extreme conditions like they were," Padraig Harrington explained, "you cannot get too result-oriented. There were plenty of good shots hit out there that didn't have good results, and you had to accept that. The key was to accept it before you hit the ball and commit to what you were doing."

Harrington thought he failed to commit just once, on his tee shot at the seventh hole, but he added: "Putting was really the hardest task out there" because the lines of the putts were changing with the gusts of the wind.

After making bogeys on the last three holes of the first nine ("I played eight and nine pretty well," he said), Harrington got the results he wanted. He posted a score of 32 on the inward nine and a round of 69 to win The Open by four strokes. He did it with a birdie on the par-4 13th hole, followed by a birdie on the 15th and an eagle on the 17th, both par-5 holes. At the 13th, Harrington hit a five iron to 15 feet from the hole. He two-putted from 40 feet at the 15th, and struck a five wood superbly at the 17th to three feet on his second shot. That provided the four-stroke margin.

Harrington felt then all he needed was to be in the fairway off the 18th tee, and he went with a three wood. "Once I hit that," he said, "I knew I had won The Open."

said. "The support I've had from my family and friends, everyone at the golf club, and all the gallery was fantastic." Alongside Jim Furyk at 10 over, after 72, Wood finished four strokes clear in the race for the Silver Medal from his fellow 20 year-old, Thomas Sherreard. The Kent amateur had pitched in from 60 yards for an eagle at the 17th and claimed a rare birdie at the 18th, a finish that to others would have bought with much gold.

Playing alongside Wood, Poulter seemed to be inspired by the energy and attention their pairing was receiving. After bogeys at two of the first three holes, birdies at the ninth and the 11th got him back to eight over and within three of the lead. A

A level-par 70 lifted Paul Casey to a tie for seventh place from a tie for 35th.

Excerpts
FROM THE Press

"By doing what major championship winners do best, Ireland's Padraig Harrington won The 137th Open at Royal Birkdale by four strokes, defending The Open title he won in a playoff last year at Carnoustie. He faltered but did not fall, stared down defeat without blinking, ignored an aching right wrist, and outlasted his opponents."

—**Larry Dorman,** *The New York Times*

"Greg Norman made the horrifying discovery at Birkdale that those who would turn back time are playing a dangerous game. Rolling back the years can also resurrect the bad days."

—**Glenn Gibbons,** *The Scotsman*

"Three years ago, when all mouth and lots of trousers, each pair louder than the next, Ian Poulter committed a fashion and golfing act of sacrilege by wearing his notorious Claret Jug strides.… His detractors … were indignant. That's the nearest he will come to the famous old trophy, they sneered. They were wrong."

—**Alan Fraser,** *Daily Mail*

"Justin Rose admitted that he was never likely to recreate the Birkdale fairytale of 10 years ago."

—**Martin Blackburn,** *The Sun*

"Simon Wakefield is a golfer with a passion for flying, and for a while he left his down-to-earth journeyman roots to soar toward the stars."

—**Mike Dickson,** *Daily Mail*

Except for a three-bogey stretch, Steve Stricker made pars on every hole.

Although Ernie Els posted a second 69, his 80 and 74 left him tied for seventh.

Justin Leonard finished 6-5 for a round of 73 to tie for 16th place.

fine chance from five feet slipped by at the 13th, and he failed to birdie the par-5 15th, but as Harrington slipped back Poulter was now only one behind. At the 16th he holed from 18 feet and now he was tied with the Irishman.

Clearly, if Poulter could post a number, with the final pairing so far without any birdies, he stood a good chance. At the 17th he found the green in two, but his first putt up the ridge finished eight feet short. He missed the birdie effort and was still at seven over. It was a crucial moment, since back at the 13th Harrington was finding his form just at the right time.

His approach from 229 yards with a five iron finished 15 feet away, pin high. What a time to hole a putt! "Any time you make a birdie in the wind it feels like getting one back on the course," he said. It was only the second 3 at the hole all day. Harrington's eyes are wonderfully expressive, but whereas at Carnoustie they had been at their most manic, now they showed nothing but assured resolve. Norman collected his third bogey in four holes and the Irishman led by one from Poulter.

Poulter needed to survive the 18th, which was playing harder than

> ### It's a
> # Fact
>
> Amateurs have won The Open on six occasions, but none since Bobby Jones in 1930. Frank Stranahan was tied second in both 1947 and 1953. Since then two of the best finishes by amateurs have been at Royal Birkdale — tied fourth in 1998 by Justin Rose and tied fifth in 2008 by Chris Wood. W D Smith was tied fifth in 1957 at St Andrews and R R Jack was tied fifth in 1959 at Muirfield.

Norman (above) reached the No 13 tee one stroke behind Harrington (right). The margin became three strokes after a bogey by Norman, after missing the fairway, and a birdie by Harrington from 15 feet.

Championship Totals	
Players Below Par	21
Players At Par	20
Players Above Par	433

Norman Treasures His 'Mini-Victories'

When Greg Norman drove out of Royal Birkdale on Sunday evening, heading for the Lake District and a short break, he hardly knew what to think of coming up just a fraction short in the final round of The Open. Sitting beside him, his wife Chris Evert remarked how it would take at least 48 hours for the enormity of what the 53 year-old golfer had just accomplished to sink in.

If Norman's 77 for a share of third place fell shy of what was required to become the oldest ever winner of a major championship, the courageous manner in which the Australian remained in contention until the last nine — he was one shot ahead of eventual winner Padraig Harrington at the turn — left the Great White Shark to remember a series of "mini-victories" rather than dwell too much on the disappointment of letting the Claret Jug slip from his grasp.

In Harrington's view, Norman had played far better golf than his closing score suggested. Indeed, the Irishman wondered how differently the last day might have turned out had Norman been the one to get up and down for par at the first rather than himself. Even when the Dubliner stood in the middle of the 17th fairway and opted to hit five wood to set up an eagle-3 rather than lay up on the par-5, he made that aggressive decision because he still feared Norman might come back at him.

By the time Norman arrived in Scotland for the Senior Open at Troon the following week, he sat down with Chrissie over a room service dinner at Turnberry Hotel and finally appreciated how his part in the 137th staging of the ancient Championship would be remembered.

"Some of the conversations I had with Chrissie, she said to me, 'the magnitude of last week will hit you 48 hours afterwards,'" he confided. "And, you know, when we sat down and had room service, you kind of sit there and go, 'Whoa, yeah, it was a really good week.' She kept all the newspapers, but I haven't read them. I wanted to reflect on it myself. You guys (the press) were great from what I hear. But I wanted to reflect on it through my own inner self rather than have somebody (influence) me with their opinions or feelings."

One point of view Norman did relish reading was an email from his old friend and rival Seve Ballesteros, who complimented the Shark on his shot-making skills at Birkdale. "I got one of best emails I've ever had from Seve," he said. "To have the reception and get the accolades, the adulation from players like Seve — he's not the only one, I just mention him because his email to me was very, very powerful — those type of things really mean a lot. That's what I meant when I said there were a lot of mini-victories. I thought on reflection, it was a very impressive performance."

Norman would not have been human, of course, had his sense of satisfaction not been tainted by regret. "Deep down inside it hurts, no question," he added. "When you're a sportsman in the arena, no matter how old or young, when you give yourself an opportunity, even though the conditions should never have happened, you still wake up and go, 'oh, no.'"

—Mike Aitken

any other day, and faced a 20-footer for par. Later, whether he holed it or not would prove academic. But not at the time, not to the player himself, who dug as deep as he ever has and slotted it home. Wood, standing alongside, said: "It was probably the best moment of the week for me. I was just so pleased for him. He is such a great player and had been such a nice guy to go round with."

"It was a great buzz all around the whole back nine," said Poulter, whose 69 put him alone at seven over. "I don't think I have enjoyed a week as much as this. ... I've done my best and it wasn't quite enough. Hats off to Padraig. Going back-to-back is very impressive. But I'll be back for lots more of this." So, too, Henrik Stenson, who closed with 71 to tie for third at nine over.

Back at the par-5 15th, Harrington two-putted for 4 and Norman, after a monster par-saver at the 14th, claimed his only birdie of the day. They both parred the 16th and then Harrington teed off with a five wood at the 17th. Norman was yet to play, and Harrington was

Low Scores	
Low First Nine	
Thomas Aiken	31
Low Second Nine	
Padraig Harrington	32
Low Round	
David Howell	67

Stephen Ames returned 71, climbing 20 places to a tie for seventh.

more worried about his playing partner, three behind, than the man two shots back in the clubhouse. His caddie, Ronan Flood, asked if he wanted to lay up, but he had a yardage of 249 and his favourite five wood in his hands. "I was worried if I laid up and made par, it would be giving Greg a chance to get within one of me with an eagle," Harrington said.

Another difficulty Harrington used to his advantage. "It was on a downslope and it is amazing how you can convince yourself under the circumstances," he said. "My ball was on a hanging lie and I said, well, this is great. It's going to come out low so I can't get it in the air. The only problem was getting it in the air for a long time." He had to allow for the wind from the left, but threaded the ball onto the green where it climbed the ridge then curved off the shoulder of the bunker on the right to three feet behind the hole.

Chris Wood had one of the best amateur finishes since 1930.

Two bogeys dropped Ben Curtis to a tie for seventh place.

It was such a fine strike that both Harrington and Flood did things they don't normally do. The player punched the air and the caddie said "Good shot" while it was still in the air.

"That's the first time I've heard him say that before the ball has finished," Harrington said. "Obviously it was a worrying shot, but I'd have been happy to be on the green and take my chances with two putts. With it three feet away, I wanted to make sure I got my four-shot lead. You can't have enough shots to play with going down 18, as I proved last year."

Norman had found trouble but made his par, while Harrington holed out for the eagle and then hit a three wood down the 18th. "Once I'd hit that, I knew I'd won The Open," he said. For good measure he hit a five-iron approach that almost went in, but by then he was already enjoying the Champion's ovation.

Adam Scott posted 72 after starting with three bogeys.

Championship Hole Summary

HOLE	PAR	YARDS	EAGLES	BIRDIES	PARS	BOGEYS	D.BOGEYS	HIGHER	RANK	AVERAGE
1	4	450	0	23	231	182	34	6	2	4.515
2	4	421	0	26	282	142	21	5	6	4.368
3	4	451	1	41	328	99	7	0	14	4.147
4	3	201	0	35	294	141	5	1	9	3.250
5	4	346	0	61	303	96	13	3	14	4.147
6	4	499	0	10	160	246	53	7	1	4.765
7	3	178	0	41	292	133	9	1	11	3.237
8	4	457	0	46	336	80	12	2	16	4.134
9	4	414	0	52	308	101	10	5	13	4.179
OUT	**34**	**3417**	**1**	**335**	**2534**	**1220**	**164**	**30**		**36.742**
10	4	408	0	29	264	148	25	9	4	4.419
11	4	436	0	27	264	143	31	9	3	4.437
12	3	184	0	31	305	121	14	3	8	3.272
13	4	499	0	25	295	135	16	3	7	4.323
14	3	201	0	28	311	125	9	1	10	3.249
15	5	544	1	92	273	85	20	3	17	5.089
16	4	439	0	27	265	155	22	5	5	4.395
17	5	572	10	191	197	64	10	2	18	4.747
18	4	473	0	38	307	114	12	3	12	4.234
IN	**36**	**3756**	**11**	**488**	**2481**	**1090**	**159**	**38**		**38.165**
TOTAL	**70**	**7173**	**12**	**823**	**5015**	**2310**	**323**	**68**		**74.907**

Harrington had a putt for par to close out the four-stroke victory (on the preceding pages). Norman (right) missed this putt on No 18 to tie for third place, then congratulated Harrington, the Champion golfer for another year.

'What a great experience it is to come down the 18th,' Harrington said.

"Ronan has been my caddie for five years," Harrington said, "and I said to him at the start that it's very special when you get to the weekend at The Open coming down the 18th, because the stands are full and everybody gets applause. Well, for the first three years I never made the weekend, and then last year we didn't get to enjoy it down the 18th, and even in the playoff we were still focused.

"This time we both thought of that at the same time, what a great experience it is to come down the 18th at The Open on the weekend with the stands full and it's even more special when you're winning The Open. The only experience that could beat it in a dramatic sense is actually holing a putt to win The Open. But there is no more comfortable or pleasurable feeling than having a four-shot lead and knowing your work is done." All that remained were two more putts.

But Harrington also had words for Norman, who closed with 77 to tie Stenson for third. "I thanked Greg for his company. He's a super guy and the perfect gentleman to be playing with in the last group of an Open," Harrington said. "He says good shot when it needs to

At the prize-giving, Harrington (above) raised the Claret Jug while Poulter (below) and Wood (bottom) were also applauded.

be said, does his own thing as well. Of course, I wanted to win, but it would have been a fantastic story if Greg had won. He has been a great champion and another win at this time in his career would have been the icing on the cake. It is never easy leading a tournament in very difficult conditions, so you have to feel for him. But, gee, you'd be happy to drive the ball like him at any stage of your career, let alone at 53 years of age."

For Norman there was an acceptance that he is no longer a full-time golfer. "I'm disappointed," he said. "Padraig played great and finished like a true Open Champion. I hung in there and can hold my head up high and I'm sure I surprised a lot of people. I thought I got off to a pretty good start, but the conditions were tough. If you haven't played a lot of golf it's hard to regroup. And I don't plan on playing too much golf."

Grinding out the practice is not on the agenda for Norman's more balanced life and, at 53 with a new bride by his side, that is fair enough. But it is exactly what brought the 36 year-old Harrington his double success. He is an Irishman with nothing to declare except his determination to work, to learn, to analyse, and to improve. Which, in its way, is genius.

Happy With His Place In History

By John Hopkins

In the aftermath of Padraig Harrington's triumph it became clear that the Irishman had perpetrated one of the greatest con tricks in the history of golf. Posing as a happy-go-lucky Irishman and a man who never believed himself worthy of a championship, never mind a major championship, he had reached a level of competence after his second victory in The Open that ranked him among the best in the world. He had done this almost without anyone noticing. That is how clever he is.

Indeed, with Tiger Woods recuperating from surgery to his left knee, Harrington had a claim to be described as the best player currently plying his trade. While Phil Mickelson was ranked second in the world immediately after The Open, one place above Harrington, he had had only one top-10 finish in major championships since the 2006 US Open, whereas Harrington had had four, of which two were victories.

How could we have so grossly underestimated Harrington that he could have ascended to this level without us really realising? Because he wanted us to, that is why. Just as he used his injured right wrist as a means of taking the pressure off him on the eve of the Championship, so he wove his own image, one that skilfully concealed the truth.

Because his name was Paddy, he had a winning smile, and he talked in sentences that were so convoluted he often ended up contradicting himself, he misled us into thinking of him as a charming Irishman and not the exceptional golfer he had become. While we had been concentrating on ephemeral matters such as his manner and his manners, we had failed to notice that Harrington had turned himself into one of the most mentally strong and skilful players in the world with a world-class short game.

Harrington at Royal Birkdale was transformed in every way from Harrington at Carnoustie. As his play seemed more thunderous this year than last, so did his character seem more impressive. This wasn't the

Harrington of six months ago, never mind 12 months ago. Gone was the relieved golfer of July 2007 who admitted that if he had not beaten Garcia in the playoff he might have given up the game.

In July 2008 he had grown so much in confidence it was almost as if he had grown physically too. He was fitter than he was a year earlier and mentally stronger. He had become a significantly better golfer, not one sneaking in to victory as those around him failed, but rather a man who struck out for the prize when the pressure was at its most fatiguing.

There are different ways of winning tournaments. You can post a score and wait until everyone has failed to meet it. You can lead after 18, 36, 54, and 72 holes and turn it into a procession. Or you can be one stroke behind after 63 holes, draw level after 64, still be level after 66, and then play the last six holes in four under par, hitting long approach strokes of at least 225 yards into all three of the greens on which you scored a birdie or an eagle. Doing it this way you shoulder your opponents aside and eventually win by four strokes.

At Carnoustie he had led going into the 72nd hole, only to nervously hit balls twice into the Barry Burn and run up 6. He thought he had lost the title, was given a second chance, and took it with both hands. Here, he took control of the Championship with his startling strike for victory at the business

end of the tournament, and from that moment the trophy was always going to be his.

The man who used to finish second many more times than win was so confident on Saturday night after the third round that he said to Bob Rotella, his sports psychologist, "I am going to win tomorrow."

Still waters run deep, they say. There isn't much still about Harrington, but his waters certainly run deep. So deep it was impossible to peer into them and see the transformation that had taken place.

Not until after his victory did we learn the things that mattered to Harrington, the things that had enabled him to improve so much. "My strengths are determination, fortitude, an ability to work things out and work through them," Harrington said. "I do not have the ability many stars have, but over the years I have learned to deal with that. Mental strength is more of a strength than talent itself.

"I've got to say that if you were to ask me my best trait over the years it has always been my ability to learn, to look around me, to see what's out there, take the best from everything, and try to put it together," Harrington continued. "I am a firm believer that those twin impostors, success and failure, are but a hair's breadth away."

In these columns last year you will have read the story of a conversation between an Irishman and a journalist on the eve of the Championship. Asked his opinion of Harrington, the journalist said he thought the Irishman had a glass jaw and that was responsible for him coming second so many times.

The same two men met by chance after that Championship and Barry the Irishman said "Good old Paddy" before adding impishly, "Pity about the glass jaw."

In this year's version of this story Barry and Declan, his friend and colleague, meet the same journalist after the Championship. "Good old Paddy" the Irishmen said as one before sticking the knife neatly between the journalist's ribs. "Pity about the glass jaw."

The Open Championship Results

Year	Champion	Score	Margin	Runners-up	Venue
1860	Willie Park Snr	174	2	Tom Morris Snr	Prestwick
1861	Tom Morris Snr	163	4	Willie Park Snr	Prestwick
1862	Tom Morris Snr	163	13	Willie Park Snr	Prestwick
1863	Willie Park Snr	168	2	Tom Morris Snr	Prestwick
1864	Tom Morris Snr	167	2	Andrew Strath	Prestwick
1865	Andrew Strath	162	2	Willie Park Snr	Prestwick
1866	Willie Park Snr	169	2	David Park	Prestwick
1867	Tom Morris Snr	170	2	Willie Park Snr	Prestwick
1868	Tom Morris Jnr	154	3	Tom Morris Snr	Prestwick
1869	Tom Morris Jnr	157	11	Bob Kirk	Prestwick
1870	Tom Morris Jnr	149	12	Bob Kirk, David Strath	Prestwick
1871	*No Competition*				
1872	Tom Morris Jnr	166	3	David Strath	Prestwick
1873	Tom Kidd	179	1	Jamie Anderson	St Andrews
1874	Mungo Park	159	2	Tom Morris Jnr	Musselburgh
1875	Willie Park Snr	166	2	Bob Martin	Prestwick
1876	Bob Martin	176	—	David Strath	St Andrews
	(Martin was awarded the title when Strath refused to play-off)				
1877	Jamie Anderson	160	2	Bob Pringle	Musselburgh
1878	Jamie Anderson	157	2	Bob Kirk	Prestwick
1879	Jamie Anderson	169	3	James Allan, Andrew Kirkaldy	St Andrews
1880	Bob Ferguson	162	5	Peter Paxton	Musselburgh
1881	Bob Ferguson	170	3	Jamie Anderson	Prestwick
1882	Bob Ferguson	171	3	Willie Fernie	St Andrews
1883	Willie Fernie	158	Playoff	Bob Ferguson	Musselburgh
1884	Jack Simpson	160	4	Douglas Rolland, Willie Fernie	Prestwick
1885	Bob Martin	171	1	Archie Simpson	St Andrews
1886	David Brown	157	2	Willie Campbell	Musselburgh
1887	Willie Park Jnr	161	1	Bob Martin	Prestwick
1888	Jack Burns	171	1	David Anderson Jnr, Ben Sayers	St Andrews
1889	Willie Park Jnr	155	Playoff	Andrew Kirkaldy	Musselburgh
1890	John Ball Jnr*	164	3	Willie Fernie, Archie Simpson	Prestwick
1891	Hugh Kirkaldy	166	2	Willie Fernie, Andrew Kirkaldy	St Andrews
	(From 1892 the competition was extended to 72 holes)				
1892	Harold Hilton*	305	3	John Ball Jnr*, Hugh Kirkaldy, Sandy Herd	Muirfield

Year	Champion	Score	Margin	Runners-up	Venue
1893	Willie Auchterlonie	322	2	John Laidlay*	Prestwick
1894	J.H. Taylor	326	5	Douglas Rolland	Royal St George's
1895	J.H. Taylor	322	4	Sandy Herd	St Andrews
1896	Harry Vardon	316	Playoff	J.H. Taylor	Muirfield
1897	Harold Hilton*	314	1	James Braid	Royal Liverpool
1898	Harry Vardon	307	1	Willie Park Jnr	Prestwick
1899	Harry Vardon	310	5	Jack White	Royal St George's
1900	J.H. Taylor	309	8	Harry Vardon	St Andrews
1901	James Braid	309	3	Harry Vardon	Muirfield
1902	Sandy Herd	307	1	Harry Vardon, James Braid	Royal Liverpool
1903	Harry Vardon	300	6	Tom Vardon	Prestwick
1904	Jack White	296	1	James Braid, J.H. Taylor	Royal St George's
1905	James Braid	318	5	J.H. Taylor, Rowland Jones	St Andrews
1906	James Braid	300	4	J.H. Taylor	Muirfield
1907	Arnaud Massy	312	2	J.H. Taylor	Royal Liverpool
1908	James Braid	291	8	Tom Ball	Prestwick
1909	J.H. Taylor	295	6	James Braid, Tom Ball	Deal
1910	James Braid	299	4	Sandy Herd	St Andrews
1911	Harry Vardon	303	Playoff	Arnaud Massy	Royal St George's
1912	Ted Ray	295	4	Harry Vardon	Muirfield
1913	J.H. Taylor	304	8	Ted Ray	Royal Liverpool
1914	Harry Vardon	306	3	J.H. Taylor	Prestwick
1915-1919	*No Championship*				
1920	George Duncan	303	2	Sandy Herd	Deal
1921	Jock Hutchison	296	Playoff	Roger Wethered*	St Andrews
1922	Walter Hagen	300	1	George Duncan, Jim Barnes	Royal St George's
1923	Arthur G. Havers	295	1	Walter Hagen	Troon
1924	Walter Hagen	301	1	Ernest Whitcombe	Royal Liverpool
1925	Jim Barnes	300	1	Archie Compston, Ted Ray	Prestwick
1926	Robert T. Jones Jnr*	291	2	Al Watrous	Royal Lytham
1927	Robert T. Jones Jnr*	285	6	Aubrey Boomer, Fred Robson	St Andrews
1928	Walter Hagen	292	2	Gene Sarazen	Royal St George's
1929	Walter Hagen	292	6	John Farrell	Muirfield

Padraig Harrington (2007, 2008)

Tom Watson (1975, 1977, 1980, 1982, 1983)

Sandy Lyle (1985)

John Daly (1995)

Ben Curtis (2003)

Year	Champion	Score	Margin	Runners-up	Venue
1930	Robert T. Jones Jnr*	291	2	Leo Diegel, Macdonald Smith	Royal Liverpool
1931	Tommy Armour	296	1	Jose Jurado	Carnoustie
1932	Gene Sarazen	283	5	Macdonald Smith	Prince's
1933	Densmore Shute	292	Playoff	Craig Wood	St Andrews
1934	Henry Cotton	283	5	Sid Brews	Royal St George's
1935	Alf Perry	283	4	Alf Padgham	Muirfield
1936	Alf Padgham	287	1	Jimmy Adams	Royal Liverpool
1937	Henry Cotton	290	2	Reg Whitcombe	Carnoustie
1938	Reg Whitcombe	295	2	Jimmy Adams	Royal St George's
1939	Richard Burton	290	2	Johnny Bulla	St Andrews
1940-1945 *No Championship*					
1946	Sam Snead	290	4	Bobby Locke, Johnny Bulla	St Andrews
1947	Fred Daly	293	1	Reg Horne, Frank Stranahan*	Royal Liverpool
1948	Henry Cotton	284	5	Fred Daly	Muirfield
1949	Bobby Locke	283	Playoff	Harry Bradshaw	Royal St George's
1950	Bobby Locke	279	2	Roberto de Vicenzo	Troon
1951	Max Faulkner	285	2	Tony Cerda	Royal Portrush
1952	Bobby Locke	287	1	Peter Thomson	Royal Lytham
1953	Ben Hogan	282	4	Frank Stranahan*, Dai Rees, Peter Thomson, Tony Cerda	Carnoustie
1954	Peter Thomson	283	1	Sid Scott, Dai Rees, Bobby Locke	Royal Birkdale
1955	Peter Thomson	281	2	Johnny Fallon	St Andrews
1956	Peter Thomson	286	3	Flory van Donck	Royal Liverpool
1957	Bobby Locke	279	3	Peter Thomson	St Andrews
1958	Peter Thomson	278	Playoff	David Thomas	Royal Lytham
1959	Gary Player	284	2	Flory van Donck, Fred Bullock	Muirfield
1960	Kel Nagle	278	1	Arnold Palmer	St Andrews
1961	Arnold Palmer	284	1	Dai Rees	Royal Birkdale
1962	Arnold Palmer	276	6	Kel Nagle	Troon
1963	Bob Charles	277	Playoff	Phil Rodgers	Royal Lytham
1964	Tony Lema	279	5	Jack Nicklaus	St Andrews
1965	Peter Thomson	285	2	Christy O'Connor, Brian Huggett	Royal Birkdale
1966	Jack Nicklaus	282	1	David Thomas, Doug Sanders	Muirfield
1967	Roberto de Vicenzo	278	2	Jack Nicklaus	Royal Liverpool
1968	Gary Player	289	2	Jack Nicklaus, Bob Charles	Carnoustie
1969	Tony Jacklin	280	2	Bob Charles	Royal Lytham
1970	Jack Nicklaus	283	Playoff	Doug Sanders	St Andrews
1971	Lee Trevino	278	1	Lu Liang Huan	Royal Birkdale

Year	Champion	Score	Margin	Runners-up	Venue
1972	Lee Trevino	278	1	Jack Nicklaus	Muirfield
1973	Tom Weiskopf	276	3	Neil Coles, Johnny Miller	Troon
1974	Gary Player	282	4	Peter Oosterhuis	Royal Lytham
1975	Tom Watson	279	Playoff	Jack Newton	Carnoustie
1976	Johnny Miller	279	6	Jack Nicklaus, Severiano Ballesteros	Royal Birkdale
1977	Tom Watson	268	1	Jack Nicklaus	Turnberry
1978	Jack Nicklaus	281	2	Simon Owen, Ben Crenshaw, Raymond Floyd, Tom Kite	St Andrews
1979	Severiano Ballesteros	283	3	Jack Nicklaus, Ben Crenshaw	Royal Lytham
1980	Tom Watson	271	4	Lee Trevino	Muirfield
1981	Bill Rogers	276	4	Bernhard Langer	Royal St George's
1982	Tom Watson	284	1	Peter Oosterhuis, Nick Price	Royal Troon
1983	Tom Watson	275	1	Hale Irwin, Andy Bean	Royal Birkdale
1984	Severiano Ballesteros	276	2	Bernhard Langer, Tom Watson	St Andrews
1985	Sandy Lyle	282	1	Payne Stewart	Royal St George's
1986	Greg Norman	280	5	Gordon J. Brand	Turnberry
1987	Nick Faldo	279	1	Rodger Davis, Paul Azinger	Muirfield
1988	Severiano Ballesteros	273	2	Nick Price	Royal Lytham
1989	Mark Calcavecchia	275	Playoff	Greg Norman, Wayne Grady	Royal Troon
1990	Nick Faldo	270	5	Mark McNulty, Payne Stewart	St Andrews
1991	Ian Baker-Finch	272	2	Mike Harwood	Royal Birkdale
1992	Nick Faldo	272	1	John Cook	Muirfield
1993	Greg Norman	267	2	Nick Faldo	Royal St George's
1994	Nick Price	268	1	Jesper Parnevik	Turnberry
1995	John Daly	282	Playoff	Costantino Rocca	St Andrews
1996	Tom Lehman	271	2	Mark McCumber, Ernie Els	Royal Lytham
1997	Justin Leonard	272	3	Jesper Parnevik, Darren Clarke	Royal Troon
1998	Mark O'Meara	280	Playoff	Brian Watts	Royal Birkdale
1999	Paul Lawrie	290	Playoff	Justin Leonard, Jean Van de Velde	Carnoustie
2000	Tiger Woods	269	8	Ernie Els, Thomas Bjorn	St Andrews
2001	David Duval	274	3	Niclas Fasth	Royal Lytham
2002	Ernie Els	278	Playoff	Thomas Levet, Stuart Appleby, Steve Elkington	Muirfield
2003	Ben Curtis	283	1	Thomas Bjorn, Vijay Singh	Royal St George's
2004	Todd Hamilton	274	Playoff	Ernie Els	Royal Troon
2005	Tiger Woods	274	5	Colin Montgomerie	St Andrews
2006	Tiger Woods	270	2	Chris DiMarco	Royal Liverpool
2007	Padraig Harrington	277	Playoff	Sergio Garcia	Carnoustie
2008	Padraig Harrington	283	4	Ian Poulter	Royal Birkdale

*Denotes amateurs

Greg Norman (1986, 1993)

Mark Calcavecchia (1989)

Ernie Els (2002)

The Open Championship Records

Most Victories

6, Harry Vardon, 1896-98-99-1903-11-14
5, James Braid, 1901-05-06-08-10; J.H. Taylor, 1894-95-1900-09-13; Peter Thomson, 1954-55-56-58-65; Tom Watson, 1975-77-80-82-83

Most Times Runner-Up or Joint Runner-Up

7, Jack Nicklaus, 1964-67-68-72-76-77-79
6, J.H. Taylor, 1896-1904-05-06-07-14

Oldest Winner

Old Tom Morris, 46 years 99 days, 1867
Harry Vardon, 44 years 41 days, 1914
Roberto de Vicenzo, 44 years 93 days, 1967

Youngest Winner

Young Tom Morris, 17 years 5 months 3 days, 1868
Willie Auchterlonie, 21 years 24 days, 1893
Severiano Ballesteros, 22 years 3 months 12 days, 1979

Mark O'Meara (1998)

Youngest and Oldest Competitor

Young Tom Morris, 14 years 4 months 25 days, 1865
Gene Sarazen, 74 years 4 months 9 days, 1976

Biggest Margin of Victory

13 strokes, Old Tom Morris, 1862
12 strokes, Young Tom Morris, 1870
11 strokes, Young Tom Morris, 1869
8 strokes, J.H. Taylor, 1900 and 1913; James Braid, 1908; Tiger Woods, 2000

Lowest Winning Aggregates

267 (66, 68, 69, 64), Greg Norman, Royal St George's, 1993
268 (68, 70, 65, 65), Tom Watson, Turnberry, 1977; (69, 66, 67, 66), Nick Price, Turnberry, 1994
269 (67, 66, 67, 69), Tiger Woods, St Andrews, 2000

Lowest Aggregates in Relation to Par

269 (19 under par), Tiger Woods, St Andrews, 2000
270 (18 under par), Nick Faldo, St Andrews, 1990; Tiger Woods, Royal Liverpool, 2006

Lowest Aggregates by Runner-Up

269 (68, 70, 65, 66), Jack Nicklaus, Turnberry, 1977; (69, 63, 70, 67), Nick Faldo, Royal St George's, 1993; (68, 66, 68, 67), Jesper Parnevik, Turnberry, 1994

Lowest Aggregates by an Amateur

281 (68, 72, 70, 71), Iain Pyman, Royal St George's, 1993; (75, 66, 70, 70), Tiger Woods, Royal Lytham, 1996

Lowest Individual Round

63, Mark Hayes, second round, Turnberry, 1977; Isao Aoki, third round, Muirfield, 1980; Greg Norman, second round, Turnberry, 1986; Paul Broadhurst, third round, St Andrews, 1990; Jodie Mudd, fourth round, Royal Birkdale, 1991; Nick Faldo, second round, and Payne Stewart, fourth round, Royal St George's, 1993

Lowest Individual Round by an Amateur

66, Frank Stranahan, fourth round, Troon, 1950; Tiger Woods, second round, Royal Lytham, 1996; Justin Rose, second round, Royal Birkdale, 1998

Lowest First Round

64, Craig Stadler, Royal Birkdale, 1983; Christy O'Connor Jnr., Royal St George's, 1985; Rodger Davis, Muirfield, 1987; Raymond Floyd and Steve Pate, Muirfield, 1992

Lowest Second Round

63, Mark Hayes, Turnberry, 1977; Greg Norman, Turnberry, 1986; Nick Faldo, Royal St George's, 1993

Lowest Third Round

63, Isao Aoki, Muirfield, 1980; Paul Broadhurst, St Andrews, 1990

Lowest Fourth Round

63, Jodie Mudd, Royal Birkdale, 1991; Payne Stewart, Royal St George's, 1993

Lowest First 36 Holes

130 (66, 64), Nick Faldo, Muirfield, 1992

Lowest Second 36 Holes

130 (65, 65), Tom Watson, Turnberry, 1977; (64, 66), Ian Baker-Finch, Royal Birkdale, 1991; (66, 64), Anders Forsbrand, Turnberry, 1994

Lowest Middle 36 Holes

130 (66, 64), Fuzzy Zoeller, Turnberry, 1994

Lowest First 54 Holes

198 (67, 67, 64), Tom Lehman, Royal Lytham, 1996
199 (67, 65, 67), Nick Faldo, St Andrews, 1990; (66, 64, 69), Nick Faldo, Muirfield, 1992

Justin Leonard (1997)

Jack Nicklaus (1966, 1970, 1978) is an RBS ambassador.

Lowest Final 54 Holes

199 (66, 67, 66), Nick Price, Turnberry, 1994

Lowest 9 Holes

28, Denis Durnian, first 9, Royal Birkdale, 1983
29, Peter Thomson and Tom Haliburton, first 9, Royal Lytham, 1958; Tony Jacklin, first 9, St Andrews, 1970; Bill Longmuir, first 9, Royal Lytham, 1979; David J. Russell, first 9, Royal Lytham, 1988; Ian Baker-Finch and Paul Broadhurst, first 9, St Andrews, 1990; Ian Baker-Finch, first 9, Royal Birkdale, 1991; Paul McGinley, first 9, Royal Lytham, 1996; Ernie Els, first 9, Muirfield, 2002; Sergio Garcia, first 9, Royal Liverpool, 2006

Successive Victories

4, Young Tom Morris, 1868-72 (no Championship in 1871).
3, Jamie Anderson, 1877-79; Bob Ferguson, 1880-82, Peter Thomson, 1954-56
2, Old Tom Morris, 1861-62; J.H. Taylor, 1894-95; Harry Vardon, 1898-99; James Braid, 1905-06; Bobby Jones, 1926-27; Walter Hagen, 1928-29; Bobby Locke, 1949-50; Arnold Palmer, 1961-62; Lee Trevino, 1971-72; Tom Watson, 1982-83; Tiger Woods, 2005-06; Padraig Harrington, 2007-08

Victories by Amateurs

3, Bobby Jones, 1926-27-30
2, Harold Hilton, 1892-97
1, John Ball, 1890
Roger Wethered lost a playoff in 1921

Champions in First Appearance

Willie Park, Prestwick, 1860; Tom Kidd, St Andrews, 1873; Mungo Park, Musselburgh, 1874; Harold Hilton, Muirfield, 1892; Jock Hutchison, St Andrews, 1921; Densmore Shute, St Andrews, 1933; Ben Hogan, Carnoustie, 1953; Tony Lema, St Andrews, 1964; Tom Watson, Carnoustie, 1975; Ben Curtis, Royal St George's, 2003

Biggest Span Between First and Last Victories

19 years, J.H. Taylor, 1894-1913
18 years, Harry Vardon, 1896-1914
15 years, Gary Player, 1959-74
14 years, Willie Park Snr, 1860-75 (no competition 1871); Henry Cotton, 1934-48

Biggest Span Between Victories

11 years, Henry Cotton, 1937-48

Champions in Three Decades

Harry Vardon, 1896, 1903, 1911
J.H. Taylor, 1894, 1900, 1913
Gary Player, 1959, 1968, 1974

Highest Number of Top-Five Finishes

16, J.H. Taylor, Jack Nicklaus
15, Harry Vardon, James Braid

Highest Number of Rounds Under Par

61, Jack Nicklaus
52, Nick Faldo
44, Tom Watson

Paul Lawrie (1999)

David Duval (2001)

Highest Number of Aggregates Under Par

14, Jack Nicklaus, Nick Faldo

Most Consecutive Rounds Under 70

7, Ernie Els, 1993-94

Outright Leader After Every Round

Ted Ray, 1912; Bobby Jones, 1927; Gene Sarazen, 1932; Henry Cotton, 1934; Tom Weiskopf, 1973; Tiger Woods, 2005

Leader After Every Round Including Ties

Harry Vardon, 1899 and 1903; J.H. Taylor, 1900; Lee Trevino, 1971; Gary Player, 1974

Record Leads (Since 1892)

After 18 holes:
4 strokes, James Braid, 1908; Bobby Jones, 1927; Henry Cotton, 1934; Christy O'Connor Jnr., 1985
After 36 holes:
9 strokes, Henry Cotton, 1934
After 54 holes:
10 strokes, Henry Cotton, 1934
7 strokes, Tony Lema, 1964

Biggest Leads by Non-Champions

After 54 holes:
5 strokes, Macdonald Smith, 1925; Jean Van de Velde, 1999

Champions with Each Round Lower Than Previous One

Jack White, 1904, Royal St George's, (80, 75, 72, 69)
James Braid, 1906, Muirfield, (77, 76, 74, 73)
Henry Cotton, 1937, Carnoustie, (74, 73, 72, 71)
Ben Hogan, 1953, Carnoustie, (73, 71, 70, 68)
Gary Player, 1959, Muirfield, (75, 71, 70, 68)

Champion with Four Rounds the Same

Densmore Shute, 1933, St Andrews, (73, 73, 73, 73) (excluding the playoff)

Biggest Variation Between Rounds of a Champion

14 strokes, Henry Cotton, 1934, second round 65, fourth round 79
11 strokes, Jack White, 1904, first round 80, fourth round 69; Greg Norman, 1986, first round 74, second round 63, third round 74

Biggest Variation Between Two Rounds

20 strokes, R.G. French, 1938, second round 71, third round 91; Colin Montgomerie, 2002, second round 64, third round 84
19 strokes, R.H. Pemberton, 1938, second round 72, third round 91
18 strokes, A. Tingey Jnr., 1923, first round 94, second round 76
17 strokes, Jack Nicklaus, 1981, first round 83, second round 66; Ian Baker-Finch, 1986, first round 86, second round 69

Todd Hamilton (2004)

Best Comeback by Champions

After 18 holes:
Harry Vardon, 1896, 11 strokes behind the leader
After 36 holes:
George Duncan, 1920, 13 strokes behind the leader
After 54 holes:
Paul Lawrie, 1999, 10 strokes behind the leader

Champions with Four Rounds Under 70

Greg Norman, 1993, Royal St George's, (66, 68, 69, 64); Nick Price, 1994, Turnberry, (69, 66, 67, 66); Tiger Woods, 2000, St Andrews, (67, 66, 67, 69)
Of non-Champions:
Ernie Els, 1993, Royal St George's, (68, 69, 69, 68); Jesper Parnevik, 1994, Turnberry, (68, 66, 68, 67); Ernie Els, 2004, Royal Troon, (69, 69, 68, 68)

Best Finishing Round by a Champion

64, Greg Norman, Royal St George's, 1993
65, Tom Watson, Turnberry, 1977; Severiano Ballesteros, Royal Lytham, 1988; Justin Leonard, Royal Troon, 1997

Worst Round by a Champion Since 1939

78, Fred Daly, third round, Royal Liverpool, 1947
76, Paul Lawrie, third round, Carnoustie, 1999

Worst Finishing Round by a Champion Since 1939

75, Sam Snead, St Andrews, 1946

Best Opening Round by a Champion

66, Peter Thomson, Royal Lytham, 1958; Nick Faldo, Muirfield, 1992; Greg Norman, Royal St George's, 1993; Tiger Woods, St Andrews, 2005

Biggest Recovery in 18 Holes by a Champion

George Duncan, Deal, 1920, was 13 strokes behind the leader, Abe Mitchell, after 36 holes and level after 54

Tom Lehman (1996)

Most Appearances

46, Gary Player
38, Jack Nicklaus

Most Appearances on Final Day (Since 1892)

32, Jack Nicklaus
31, Alex Herd
30, J.H. Taylor
27, Harry Vardon, James Braid, Nick Faldo
26, Peter Thomson, Gary Player
23, Dai Rees
22, Henry Cotton

Most Appearances Before First Victory

16, Nick Price, 1994
14, Mark O'Meara, 1998

Most Appearances Without a Victory

29, Dai Rees
28, Sam Torrance
27, Neil Coles

Championship with Highest Number of Rounds Under 70

148, Turnberry, 1994

Championship Since 1946 with the Fewest Rounds Under 70

St Andrews, 1946; Royal Liverpool, 1947; Royal Portrush, 1951; Royal Liverpool, 1956; Carnoustie, 1968. All had only two rounds under 70.

Longest Course

Carnoustie, 2007, 7421 yards

Courses Most Often Used

St Andrews, 27; Prestwick, 24; Muirfield, 15; Royal St George's, 13; Royal Liverpool, 11; Royal Lytham, 10; Royal Birkdale, 9; Royal Troon, 8; Carnoustie, 7; Musselburgh, 6; Turnberry, 3; Deal, 2; Royal Portrush and Prince's, 1

Prize Money

Year	Total	First Prize
1860	nil	nil
1863	10	nil
1864	15	6
1876	27	10
1889	22	8
1891	30.50	10
1892	100	35
1893	100	30
1910	135	50
1920	225	75
1927	275	75
1930	400	100
1931	500	100
1946	1,000	150
1949	1,500	300
1953	2,500	500
1954	3,500	750
1955	3,750	1,000
1958	4,850	1,000
1959	5,000	1,000
1960	7,000	1,250
1961	8,500	1,400
1963	8,500	1,500
1965	10,000	1,750
1966	15,000	2,100
1968	20,000	3,000
1969	30,334	4,250
1970	40,000	5,250
1971	45,000	5,500
1972	50,000	5,500
1975	75,000	7,500
1977	100,000	10,000
1978	125,000	12,500
1979	155,000	15,000
1980	200,000	25,000
1982	250,000	32,000
1983	310,000	40,000
1984	445,000	50,000
1985	530,000	65,000
1986	634,000	70,000
1987	650,000	75,000
1988	700,000	80,000
1989	750,000	80,000
1990	825,000	85,000

Year	Total	First Prize
1991	900,000	90,000
1992	950,000	95,000
1993	1,000,000	100,000
1994	1,100,000	110,000
1995	1,250,000	125,000
1996	1,400,000	200,000
1997	1,586,300	250,000
1998	1,800,000	300,000

Year	Total	First Prize
1999	2,000,000	350,000
2000	2,750,000	500,000
2001	3,300,000	600,000
2002	3,800,000	700,000
2003	3,900,000	700,000
2004	4,000,000	720,000
2007	4,200,000	750,000

Attendance

Year	Total	Year	Total	Year	Total
1962	37,098	1978	125,271	1993	141,000
1963	24,585	1979	134,501	1994	128,000
1964	35,954			1995	180,000
1965	32,927	1980	131,610	1996	170,000
1966	40,182	1981	111,987	1997	176,000
1967	29,880	1982	133,299	1998	195,100
1968	51,819	1983	142,892	1999	157,000
1969	46,001	1984	193,126		
		1985	141,619	2000	238,787
1970	81,593	1986	134,261	2001	178,000
1971	70,076	1987	139,189	2002	161,500
1972	84,746	1988	191,334	2003	183,000
1973	78,810	1989	160,639	2004	176,000
1974	92,796			2005	223,000
1975	85,258	1990	208,680	2006	230,000
1976	92,021	1991	189,435	2007	154,000
1977	87,615	1992	146,427	2008	201,500

The 137th Open Championship

Complete Scores

HOLE			1	2	3	4	5	6	7	8	9	10	11	12	13	14	15	16	17	18	
PAR	POSITION		4	4	4	3	4	3	4	4	4	4	4	3	4	3	5	4	5	4	TOTAL
Padraig Harrington	T38	Round 1	5	4	4	4	3	5	3	3	4	4	5	3	4	3	5	4	6	5	74
Republic of Ireland	T4	Round 2	4	3	4	3	4	5	3	4	4	5	5	3	4	3	4	4	3	3	68
£750,000	T2	Round 3	4	5	4	3	3	4	2	5	4	4	5	5	4	3	4	5	4	4	72
	1	Round 4	4	4	4	3	4	4	4	5	5	4	4	3	3	3	4	4	3	4	**69 -283**
Ian Poulter	T15	Round 1	4	4	5	3	3	5	4	4	3	4	5	4	4	4	4	4	4	4	72
England	T11	Round 2	4	4	4	4	3	4	3	4	4	4	4	3	5	4	5	4	4	4	71
£450,000	T9	Round 3	4	4	4	4	4	5	3	4	4	4	4	4	3	6	4	6	4	4	75
	2	Round 4	5	4	5	3	4	4	3	4	3	4	3	3	4	3	5	3	5	4	**69 -287**
Henrik Stenson	T74	Round 1	4	4	4	3	4	5	4	4	5	4	5	3	5	4	5	4	4	5	76
Sweden	T52	Round 2	5	4	4	3	4	4	4	4	5	4	3	3	4	3	5	4	5	4	72
£255,000	T9	Round 3	5	4	4	3	4	4	3	4	3	4	4	3	4	3	4	6	4	4	70
	T3	Round 4	5	4	4	3	4	5	3	4	3	4	4	3	4	4	4	4	4	5	**71 -289**
Greg Norman	T4	Round 1	5	4	3	3	4	4	3	4	4	4	4	3	5	3	5	4	4	4	70
Australia	2	Round 2	3	4	4	3	4	6	2	3	4	4	4	3	4	3	5	4	6	4	70
£255,000	1	Round 3	5	4	5	3	4	5	3	3	4	6	4	3	4	2	5	4	4	4	72
	T3	Round 4	5	5	5	3	4	5	3	4	4	5	4	4	5	3	4	4	5	5	**77 -289**
Jim Furyk	T7	Round 1	5	5	4	3	5	4	3	4	4	4	4	3	4	2	5	4	4	4	71
USA	T4	Round 2	4	4	4	3	4	5	3	3	4	4	5	2	5	3	5	4	5	4	71
£180,000	T15	Round 3	4	4	4	4	4	5	3	3	3	6	5	4	4	5	5	4	5	5	77
	T5	Round 4	5	5	4	3	4	4	3	4	4	4	4	3	4	3	4	4	5	4	**71 -290**
Chris Wood*	T52	Round 1	4	4	5	3	4	6	3	4	4	4	5	3	4	3	5	4	5	5	75
England	T22	Round 2	5	4	4	3	3	5	3	3	4	4	4	3	4	3	5	5	5	3	70
	T9	Round 3	5	5	4	3	4	5	3	4	4	5	4	4	3	3	5	4	4	4	73
	T5	Round 4	4	4	5	3	4	4	2	4	3	4	5	4	5	3	5	4	4	5	**72 -290**
David Howell	T74	Round 1	5	5	5	4	4	5	3	5	5	3	5	2	4	3	5	5	4	4	76
England	T38	Round 2	4	4	4	3	4	5	3	4	4	5	4	3	4	3	5	4	4	4	71
£96,944	T64	Round 3	5	5	4	4	4	4	4	4	4	4	4	4	4	4	7	5	4	4	78
	T7	Round 4	4	4	5	3	3	4	2	4	4	4	3	4	4	3	4	4	3	5	**67 -292**
Robert Karlsson	T52	Round 1	3	4	4	3	4	5	4	4	4	4	4	4	4	4	6	4	5	4	75
Sweden	T52	Round 2	4	5	4	2	3	5	3	4	4	4	4	3	5	3	5	5	5	4	73
£96,944	T48	Round 3	4	4	4	3	4	6	3	4	4	5	5	4	3	4	5	4	5	4	75
	T7	Round 4	3	4	4	3	4	4	3	4	4	5	3	3	4	3	5	5	4	4	**69 -292**

* Denotes amateurs

HOLE		1	2	3	4	5	6	7	8	9	10	11	12	13	14	15	16	17	18	
PAR	POSITION	4	4	4	3	4	4	3	4	4	4	4	3	4	3	5	4	5	4	TOTAL
Ernie Els	T136 Round 1	4	4	4	3	4	5	3	4	4	5	4	4	4	6	6	6	5	5	80
South Africa	T69 Round 2	4	4	3	4	5	3	3	4	4	3	5	2	4	4	4	4	4	5	69
£96,944	T48 Round 3	5	4	4	4	5	4	4	4	4	4	4	3	4	2	4	5	6	4	74
	T7 Round 4	4	4	4	2	4	4	3	4	4	5	4	3	4	3	4	4	5	4	69 -292
Paul Casey	T110 Round 1	4	5	4	3	6	5	4	4	5	4	4	3	4	4	5	5	5	4	78
England	T69 Round 2	5	5	4	3	4	5	3	4	5	4	3	3	3	2	5	5	4	4	71
£96,944	T35 Round 3	6	4	4	3	4	4	2	3	4	5	4	3	4	4	7	4	5	3	73
	T7 Round 4	4	4	4	4	4	4	3	4	4	5	5	3	4	3	3	4	4	4	70 -292
Stephen Ames	T27 Round 1	6	4	3	3	4	4	4	4	4	4	4	3	4	4	5	5	5	3	73
Canada	T11 Round 2	5	3	4	3	4	5	3	3	4	5	4	4	4	3	4	4	5	3	70
£96,944	T27 Round 3	6	4	4	4	5	6	3	3	5	7	3	3	5	3	5	3	5	4	78
	T7 Round 4	4	5	5	3	3	4	3	3	4	5	4	3	4	3	5	4	5	4	71 -292
Steve Stricker	T91 Round 1	4	5	4	4	5	5	3	4	4	5	5	3	5	4	5	5	5	3	77
USA	T52 Round 2	4	4	4	4	5	5	3	4	3	4	4	3	4	3	5	4	4	4	71
£96,944	T15 Round 3	4	4	4	3	4	5	3	4	4	4	4	4	4	3	5	4	4	4	71
	T7 Round 4	4	4	4	3	5	5	4	4	4	4	4	3	4	3	5	4	5	4	73 -292
Robert Allenby	T1 Round 1	5	4	4	3	4	5	4	4	4	3	4	2	4	3	5	4	4	3	69
Australia	T4 Round 2	5	5	4	3	4	4	4	4	5	4	4	3	4	4	4	4	4	4	73
£96,944	T9 Round 3	5	4	5	3	4	5	3	4	4	5	4	4	4	3	6	4	4	5	76
	T7 Round 4	3	5	4	3	4	7	3	4	4	5	4	3	5	3	6	4	3	4	74 -292
Anthony Kim	T15 Round 1	4	4	3	4	4	4	3	5	4	5	4	3	4	4	4	5	4	4	72
USA	T27 Round 2	4	5	4	3	4	6	3	4	4	4	4	3	4	2	6	4	5	5	74
£96,944	T5 Round 3	4	4	5	4	4	5	3	4	4	4	4	3	4	3	5	4	3	4	71
	T7 Round 4	4	4	4	3	4	5	3	4	4	5	3	4	3	5	5	6	5	5	75 -292
Ben Curtis	T110 Round 1	7	6	4	3	4	5	4	4	4	4	5	3	3	3	6	4	5	4	78
USA	T38 Round 2	3	4	4	4	4	4	3	4	5	3	4	3	4	3	5	4	4	4	69
£96,944	T5 Round 3	4	4	2	3	3	5	2	4	4	4	5	4	5	3	5	4	5	4	70
	T7 Round 4	5	3	5	3	4	4	3	5	4	4	4	4	5	3	4	4	6	5	75 -292
Adam Scott	T4 Round 1	4	4	4	3	4	3	3	4	4	4	4	3	4	3	4	5	6	4	70
Australia	T16 Round 2	4	5	3	3	4	4	4	4	5	4	5	3	5	3	5	4	4	5	74
£53,167	T27 Round 3	5	6	4	2	4	5	2	4	5	6	4	3	5	3	7	4	4	4	77
	T16 Round 4	5	5	5	2	4	4	2	5	4	5	3	4	4	3	4	4	5	4	72 -293
Justin Leonard	T91 Round 1	4	6	4	3	4	4	3	4	5	5	5	3	4	3	5	5	6	4	77
USA	T38 Round 2	5	4	3	3	4	4	3	5	3	3	5	3	6	3	4	4	4	4	70
£53,167	T20 Round 3	5	5	4	3	4	6	3	4	4	4	4	4	4	3	5	3	4	4	73
	T16 Round 4	4	3	4	4	4	5	4	3	4	4	4	3	4	3	5	4	6	5	73 -293
KJ Choi	T15 Round 1	4	4	4	2	5	4	3	4	4	5	4	3	5	3	5	5	5	4	72
South Korea	1 Round 2	5	4	3	3	4	4	3	4	4	4	4	3	3	3	5	4	4	3	67
£53,167	T2 Round 3	4	4	4	3	4	6	3	5	4	6	4	3	3	3	6	4	5	4	75
	T16 Round 4	5	4	4	4	5	5	4	5	4	4	5	3	4	3	5	3	4	8	79 -293
Jean Van de Velde	T27 Round 1	5	4	4	3	4	4	2	4	4	5	5	3	5	3	5	5	4	4	73
France	T16 Round 2	3	4	4	3	4	4	2	4	4	4	6	2	4	3	7	4	5	4	71
£37,771	T59 Round 3	5	4	5	5	5	5	3	4	4	6	6	3	4	3	6	4	3	5	80
	T19 Round 4	4	4	5	3	3	4	3	5	4	4	3	3	4	3	5	3	6	4	70 -294
Gregory Havret	T7 Round 1	4	4	4	4	4	4	4	4	4	4	5	3	4	3	4	5	3	4	71
France	T27 Round 2	5	5	3	3	4	5	4	4	4	4	4	3	5	3	4	5	5	5	75
£37,771	T48 Round 3	4	4	4	4	4	5	4	4	4	4	7	3	4	3	6	4	5	4	77
	T19 Round 4	5	3	3	4	5	4	3	4	3	4	4	3	6	3	5	4	5	3	71 -294
Paul Waring	T27 Round 1	4	4	5	2	4	5	4	4	4	5	5	4	4	3	5	3	5	3	73
England	T38 Round 2	5	4	4	3	5	4	4	3	4	4	5	3	4	4	5	4	4	5	74
£37,771	T48 Round 3	4	5	6	3	4	4	3	4	4	6	4	4	5	4	5	3	4	4	76
	T19 Round 4	4	3	3	3	5	4	3	4	3	5	6	3	4	3	5	4	5	4	71 -294

HOLE			1	2	3	4	5	6	7	8	9	10	11	12	13	14	15	16	17	18	
PAR	POSITION		4	4	4	3	4	4	3	4	4	4	4	3	4	3	5	4	5	4	TOTAL
Phil Mickelson	T123	Round 1	5	5	4	4	4	7	3	5	4	5	4	3	4	3	4	5	6	4	79
USA	T38	Round 2	4	4	4	3	4	4	4	4	3	4	4	3	4	2	5	4	5	3	68
£37,771	T48	Round 3	4	5	4	4	4	4	3	4	4	5	5	4	4	4	4	5	5	4	76
	T19	Round 4	4	4	5	3	4	5	3	4	4	4	4	4	4	3	4	4	4	4	71 -294
Graeme McDowell	T1	Round 1	4	4	4	3	4	5	3	4	4	4	4	3	4	3	5	4	4	3	69
Northern Ireland	T4	Round 2	4	5	4	3	4	5	3	4	4	5	5	3	4	3	5	3	5	4	73
£37,771	T59	Round 3	6	4	5	3	3	5	3	4	5	4	4	3	5	4	5	6	5	6	80
	T19	Round 4	4	4	4	2	4	5	3	4	4	4	4	3	5	4	5	4	5	4	72 -294
Fredrik Jacobson	T7	Round 1	6	4	4	3	4	5	2	4	4	4	3	3	3	3	5	4	4	5	71
Sweden	T11	Round 2	4	5	3	3	3	4	4	4	4	4	4	3	4	4	5	5	5	4	72
£37,771	T35	Round 3	5	5	5	3	4	4	3	5	4	4	3	4	7	3	5	5	5	5	79
	T19	Round 4	4	4	4	3	4	3	4	4	4	4	4	3	4	3	6	4	4	6	72 -294
Thomas Sherreard*	T91	Round 1	4	5	4	3	5	5	3	4	4	5	4	5	4	3	5	4	5	5	77
England	T27	Round 2	4	4	4	3	3	5	3	3	4	4	4	3	4	4	4	4	5	4	69
	T48	Round 3	6	4	4	3	4	5	3	4	4	5	4	3	4	3	6	4	5	5	76
	T19	Round 4	4	4	4	4	5	5	4	4	4	5	4	3	4	3	5	4	3	3	72 -294
Trevor Immelman	T38	Round 1	5	4	4	2	5	4	4	4	4	6	5	3	5	3	4	4	4	4	74
South Africa	T52	Round 2	4	4	4	3	4	5	3	4	5	4	6	3	4	3	5	5	4	4	74
£37,771	T27	Round 3	5	4	3	4	4	6	4	4	4	4	4	3	4	2	6	4	4	4	73
	T19	Round 4	4	3	4	3	5	4	4	3	4	5	4	3	6	3	5	4	5	4	73 -294
Anders Hansen	T110	Round 1	4	5	5	4	4	6	3	3	3	5	6	4	4	3	5	5	5	4	78
Denmark	T27	Round 2	4	3	4	3	4	4	2	4	3	4	4	3	5	3	4	5	4	5	68
£37,771	T20	Round 3	4	4	3	4	4	5	4	4	3	5	4	4	4	3	6	4	4	5	74
	T19	Round 4	4	3	4	4	4	6	3	4	5	5	4	2	5	4	4	4	4	5	74 -294
Davis Love III	T52	Round 1	4	5	4	3	4	6	4	4	4	4	4	3	4	3	5	5	5	4	75
USA	T69	Round 2	4	4	6	3	3	6	3	4	4	4	5	3	4	3	5	4	5	4	74
£37,771	T15	Round 3	4	4	4	3	4	4	3	4	4	5	3	4	3	5	4	4	4	4	70
	T19	Round 4	5	5	4	4	4	5	3	4	5	4	3	4	3	5	4	5	5	5	75 -294
Rocco Mediate	T1	Round 1	5	4	5	3	5	4	3	3	4	4	4	3	3	3	5	4	4	3	69
USA	T4	Round 2	4	4	4	3	4	5	2	4	4	4	6	3	4	4	5	4	6	3	73
£37,771	T9	Round 3	6	4	4	4	4	5	4	3	5	4	4	4	5	3	5	4	4	4	76
	T19	Round 4	5	6	4	3	4	4	4	5	3	5	4	3	5	3	5	4	5	4	76 -294
Alexander Noren	T15	Round 1	6	4	4	3	4	4	3	4	4	3	4	4	4	3	5	4	4	5	72
Sweden	T4	Round 2	4	5	4	3	4	5	2	4	4	4	5	3	4	2	5	4	4	4	70
£37,771	T5	Round 3	5	7	4	3	4	4	3	4	4	4	4	4	5	3	4	4	5	4	75
	T19	Round 4	4	4	4	4	4	5	4	5	4	5	4	4	4	3	4	4	5	6	77 -294
Simon Wakefield	T7	Round 1	4	5	5	3	5	4	3	4	3	4	4	3	4	3	5	4	4	4	71
England	T22	Round 2	3	4	4	3	4	4	4	4	5	5	6	4	4	3	5	4	4	4	74
£37,771	4	Round 3	4	4	4	4	4	5	3	4	4	4	4	2	5	2	5	4	4	4	70
	T19	Round 4	5	4	4	3	3	5	4	4	4	5	4	4	5	3	6	4	8	4	79 -294
Richard Green	T74	Round 1	5	5	4	3	4	5	4	4	5	5	4	4	4	4	4	5	4	3	76
Australia	T52	Round 2	4	4	5	3	4	4	3	4	4	5	3	3	4	3	5	5	5	4	72
£25,036	T59	Round 3	4	5	5	3	4	4	3	4	4	4	4	3	5	3	6	5	6	4	76
	T32	Round 4	5	4	4	3	4	5	3	3	4	4	5	3	4	3	5	4	4	4	71 -295
Andres Romero	T91	Round 1	4	6	4	3	4	5	3	4	4	5	4	4	4	3	5	6	5	4	77
Argentina	T69	Round 2	5	4	4	3	4	5	3	4	4	4	5	2	4	3	5	5	4	4	72
£25,036	T48	Round 3	4	4	3	3	4	5	3	4	4	4	4	4	4	5	5	5	5	4	74
	T32	Round 4	4	3	5	3	4	4	4	4	4	6	4	3	4	3	4	4	4	5	72 -295
Nick O'Hern	T38	Round 1	5	5	4	3	3	5	3	5	4	4	3	4	4	4	6	3	5	4	74
Australia	T69	Round 2	5	4	4	3	4	5	4	4	4	4	4	4	5	3	5	4	5	4	75
£25,036	T48	Round 3	4	5	4	4	4	4	3	4	5	4	4	3	4	3	5	4	6	4	74
	T32	Round 4	4	3	4	4	4	4	3	3	4	5	4	3	4	3	5	4	6	5	72 -295

HOLE		1	2	3	4	5	6	7	8	9	10	11	12	13	14	15	16	17	18	
PAR	POSITION	4	4	4	3	4	4	3	4	4	4	4	3	4	3	5	4	5	4	TOTAL
Heath Slocum	T27	Round 1	4	4	5	2	4	5	3	4	4	4	4	4	5	3	5	5	4	4	73
USA	T69	Round 2	3	4	4	3	4	5	3	4	4	4	5	3	6	3	6	5	5	5	76
£25,036	T48	Round 3	5	4	4	3	4	5	3	4	5	4	4	3	4	3	4	5	4	6	74
	T32	Round 4	5	4	4	3	3	5	3	4	4	4	3	3	5	4	5	4	5	4	72 **-295**
Tom Lehman	T38	Round 1	5	4	4	3	3	4	4	4	3	4	4	3	4	4	8	4	5	4	74
USA	T38	Round 2	4	4	4	3	4	4	3	4	4	4	4	3	4	4	6	5	5	4	73
£25,036	T20	Round 3	4	4	4	2	5	3	4	5	5	4	4	4	4	4	4	4	4	5	73
	T32	Round 4	4	4	3	4	4	6	3	5	4	5	5	2	4	3	4	4	6	5	75 **-295**
Todd Hamilton	T38	Round 1	4	5	5	2	4	5	4	4	4	5	4	3	4	2	5	4	6	4	74
USA	T52	Round 2	5	5	4	3	4	5	3	3	5	4	4	3	4	3	5	4	6	4	74
£25,036	T20	Round 3	4	4	4	4	4	5	3	3	4	4	4	4	3	6	4	4	4	4	72
	T32	Round 4	4	4	4	4	4	5	3	4	4	4	4	3	4	4	5	4	6	5	75 **-295**
Retief Goosen	T7	Round 1	4	4	4	3	6	4	3	4	3	4	4	2	4	2	6	5	4	5	71
South Africa	T27	Round 2	4	4	4	3	4	5	2	4	5	5	4	3	5	2	6	5	6	4	75
£25,036	T15	Round 3	5	4	4	4	3	4	2	4	3	5	4	4	5	3	5	6	4	4	73
	T32	Round 4	5	4	4	4	4	5	4	5	4	4	5	3	4	3	5	3	5	5	76 **-295**
Thomas Aiken	T52	Round 1	5	5	5	4	4	5	4	3	5	3	4	2	4	3	6	4	5	4	75
South Africa	T27	Round 2	5	5	3	3	4	4	3	3	4	4	4	3	4	4	5	5	4	4	71
£16,646	T79	Round 3	5	4	4	3	5	5	3	4	4	5	8	6	5	3	6	4	4	4	82
	T39	Round 4	4	4	4	3	4	4	2	3	3	4	4	3	5	3	5	5	4	4	68 **-296**
David Duval	T27	Round 1	5	4	4	4	3	5	3	4	4	5	4	2	4	3	5	5	4	5	73
USA	T4	Round 2	3	4	4	3	4	5	3	4	4	3	3	3	5	2	5	5	5	4	69
£16,646	T64	Round 3	7	5	5	4	4	6	4	5	4	5	4	4	4	3	5	4	5	5	83
	T39	Round 4	5	3	3	3	3	4	3	4	5	5	3	4	3	6	4	4	4	5	71 **-296**
Areil Canete	T110	Round 1	4	5	4	3	5	7	3	5	5	4	4	4	4	4	3	5	5	4	78
Argentina	T69	Round 2	4	4	4	3	4	4	3	4	5	4	4	3	4	4	4	5	4	4	71
£16,646	T64	Round 3	5	4	4	4	4	5	4	5	4	5	4	3	4	4	4	5	4	4	76
	T39	Round 4	6	4	4	3	4	3	2	5	4	5	4	3	4	3	4	4	5	4	71 **-296**
Gregory Bourdy	T38	Round 1	4	4	4	3	7	4	3	4	4	4	4	3	4	3	5	4	6	4	74
France	T52	Round 2	5	4	4	4	4	4	3	5	3	4	5	4	4	3	5	4	4	5	74
£16,646	T48	Round 3	5	4	4	3	4	6	3	4	4	4	5	3	5	3	5	4	5	4	75
	T39	Round 4	5	4	4	3	4	5	3	4	3	4	4	3	4	3	4	5	7	4	73 **-296**
Jay Williamson	T27	Round 1	4	5	4	3	4	5	4	4	4	4	3	5	3	3	6	3	5	4	73
USA	T22	Round 2	4	4	4	3	5	4	3	4	3	4	4	4	5	3	5	4	5	4	72
£16,646	T35	Round 3	3	4	4	4	5	5	4	7	4	5	5	4	4	3	5	4	4	3	77
	T39	Round 4	5	4	4	3	6	5	4	4	4	4	4	3	4	3	4	4	5	4	74 **-296**
Woody Austin	T74	Round 1	5	3	4	3	4	4	4	4	5	6	4	3	4	3	6	6	4	4	76
USA	T52	Round 2	4	4	4	3	4	5	3	4	4	4	4	3	4	3	6	4	5	4	72
£16,646	T35	Round 3	5	4	6	4	4	5	3	4	4	4	4	3	4	3	5	3	5	4	74
	T39	Round 4	4	4	5	3	6	5	3	3	5	4	3	4	4	3	5	4	5	4	74 **-296**
Bart Bryant	T4	Round 1	4	4	4	3	4	5	3	4	4	4	3	3	4	3	6	4	5	3	70
USA	T52	Round 2	5	4	5	4	4	5	4	4	5	4	4	4	4	3	6	4	5	4	78
£16,646	T35	Round 3	5	6	5	3	3	5	3	4	3	4	4	4	4	3	5	4	5	4	74
	T39	Round 4	4	5	5	4	4	4	3	4	4	5	4	3	4	3	5	5	4	4	74 **-296**
Mike Weir	T7	Round 1	5	4	4	3	3	6	3	4	4	4	4	3	3	3	5	6	3	4	71
Canada	T38	Round 2	4	5	4	3	4	5	3	4	4	4	4	2	5	3	8	5	5	4	76
£16,646	T27	Round 3	6	4	3	4	3	5	4	4	4	4	4	3	5	3	5	3	5	5	74
	T39	Round 4	5	4	4	3	4	5	2	6	4	4	4	3	4	4	5	5	5	4	75 **-296**
Camilo Villegas	T74	Round 1	4	4	5	3	4	6	4	4	4	4	4	3	4	4	5	5	5	4	76
Colombia	3	Round 2	5	5	4	2	3	4	3	4	3	4	4	3	5	2	4	3	4	3	65
£16,646	T20	Round 3	5	4	4	4	4	4	4	4	5	6	4	4	6	4	4	4	5	4	79
	T39	Round 4	5	3	4	4	4	4	3	5	4	4	7	3	4	2	5	5	6	4	76 **-296**

HOLE			1	2	3	4	5	6	7	8	9	10	11	12	13	14	15	16	17	18	
PAR	POSITION		4	4	4	3	4	4	3	4	4	4	4	3	4	3	5	4	5	4	TOTAL
Simon Khan	T91	Round 1	7	4	4	3	5	6	3	4	3	4	4	5	4	4	5	4	4	4	77
England	T69	Round 2	5	3	3	4	6	4	4	4	4	3	4	3	4	3	6	4	4	4	72
£16,646	T20	Round 3	4	3	5	3	5	4	3	4	4	4	5	4	4	3	5	3	4	4	71
	T39	Round 4	5	4	4	3	4	6	3	4	4	4	5	4	4	4	5	4	4	5	76 **-296**
Graeme Storm	T74	Round 1	4	4	5	3	4	4	4	4	4	4	5	3	5	3	5	5	5	5	76
England	T27	Round 2	4	4	5	3	4	4	3	5	4	3	3	3	4	3	5	4	5	4	70
£16,646	T9	Round 3	4	4	3	3	4	5	4	4	4	4	4	4	4	4	5	4	4	4	72
	T39	Round 4	5	5	4	3	3	4	3	4	5	5	5	3	4	4	6	5	5	5	78 **-296**
Ross Fisher	T15	Round 1	4	4	4	3	4	4	4	4	4	4	5	3	4	4	4	4	5	4	72
England	T27	Round 2	5	4	4	3	4	5	3	4	5	4	4	4	3	5	4	4	5	74
£16,646	T5	Round 3	4	5	4	3	4	4	3	4	5	6	3	3	4	2	5	4	4	4	71
	T39	Round 4	4	4	4	4	4	5	3	4	4	5	5	4	4	4	5	4	4	8	79 **-296**
Anthony Wall	T7	Round 1	3	4	4	4	4	5	3	4	4	3	5	4	4	3	4	4	5	4	71
England	T16	Round 2	3	4	5	4	4	4	3	4	4	5	4	3	4	3	6	4	5	4	73
£11,786	T64	Round 3	5	5	5	3	4	5	5	4	4	4	4	5	5	3	6	4	6	4	81
	T51	Round 4	4	4	5	3	4	5	3	4	4	4	4	3	4	3	5	4	4	5	72 **-297**
Michael Campbell	T52	Round 1	5	4	4	2	5	6	2	4	5	5	3	3	4	4	6	4	5	4	75
New Zealand	T69	Round 2	5	4	4	3	5	4	3	3	5	6	4	3	4	3	5	4	4	4	74
£11,786	T48	Round 3	4	5	4	3	4	5	2	5	4	4	4	3	4	3	6	5	5	4	74
	T51	Round 4	4	4	5	3	4	5	4	4	3	4	7	3	4	3	5	4	4	4	74 **-297**
Stuart Appleby	T15	Round 1	4	4	4	3	4	5	4	4	4	5	4	3	4	3	5	4	5	3	72
Australia	T11	Round 2	4	4	4	4	5	5	4	3	4	3	4	3	4	3	5	4	4	4	71
£11,786	T35	Round 3	4	4	5	3	4	5	2	5	4	7	4	4	4	4	5	5	5	5	79
	T51	Round 4	4	4	4	4	4	4	3	5	4	5	4	3	5	4	5	4	5	4	75 **-297**
Doug Labelle II	T110	Round 1	4	5	4	3	5	5	3	4	5	5	7	3	4	3	5	4	4	5	78
USA	T52	Round 2	5	3	4	3	4	6	3	4	4	4	4	3	5	3	4	3	4	4	70
£11,786	T35	Round 3	5	4	4	3	4	4	4	4	5	4	4	3	3	4	6	4	5	4	74
	T51	Round 4	5	5	4	3	4	4	3	5	4	4	5	4	4	3	5	4	4	5	75 **-297**
Zach Johnson	T27	Round 1	5	5	4	2	4	5	2	4	4	4	5	3	4	4	6	5	3	73
USA	T22	Round 2	4	4	4	3	5	4	3	4	4	4	5	3	4	3	4	4	6	4	72
£11,786	T27	Round 3	5	5	4	3	4	6	3	4	5	5	3	3	4	3	5	5	5	4	76
	T51	Round 4	6	4	4	5	4	5	3	4	3	4	4	3	4	3	5	4	6	5	76 **-297**
David Frost	T52	Round 1	5	4	4	3	5	5	3	4	4	4	5	2	4	3	5	5	5	5	75
South Africa	T52	Round 2	4	5	5	3	4	5	3	4	3	5	4	2	5	2	6	4	4	5	73
£11,786	T27	Round 3	4	4	4	3	4	4	3	5	4	4	4	5	3	5	5	4	4	73
	T51	Round 4	6	6	5	3	4	6	4	4	4	4	4	4	3	3	4	4	4	4	76 **-297**
Sergio Garcia	T15	Round 1	5	4	4	3	4	5	3	4	4	5	4	3	4	3	4	4	5	4	72
Spain	T22	Round 2	5	4	4	2	4	4	3	4	4	5	6	3	4	3	5	4	4	5	73
£11,786	T15	Round 3	4	5	4	3	5	4	3	5	4	5	4	3	3	3	5	5	4	5	74
	T51	Round 4	5	4	4	3	4	4	3	4	3	5	5	4	6	5	5	4	5	5	78 **-297**
Richard Finch	T52	Round 1	5	6	5	4	5	4	2	4	4	4	4	3	4	3	5	5	4	4	75
England	T52	Round 2	4	5	4	3	4	4	3	4	4	4	4	3	4	3	5	5	6	4	73
£10,650	T73	Round 3	4	5	4	4	5	4	3	6	4	4	4	4	5	2	6	4	5	5	78
	T58	Round 4	5	4	4	2	4	4	2	4	3	7	4	3	4	3	5	4	6	4	72 **-298**
Tom Gillis	T38	Round 1	5	5	5	3	5	4	4	4	4	4	4	4	5	3	4	4	4	3	74
USA	T27	Round 2	5	4	4	4	4	4	3	4	4	4	4	4	4	3	5	4	4	4	72
£10,650	T64	Round 3	5	5	4	5	4	4	3	5	3	4	4	4	3	4	6	5	6	5	79
	T58	Round 4	4	4	5	3	5	5	3	4	4	5	4	2	4	3	5	4	5	4	73 **-298**
Kevin Stadler	T15	Round 1	4	5	4	4	4	5	3	3	4	3	6	3	4	3	5	4	4	4	72
USA	T38	Round 2	4	4	4	3	4	4	4	4	5	4	7	3	5	4	4	4	4	4	75
£10,650	T64	Round 3	4	5	5	4	4	5	4	4	4	4	5	4	4	5	5	4	4	4	78
	T58	Round 4	4	4	4	3	4	5	2	4	4	5	4	2	4	4	7	4	5	4	73 **-298**

HOLE			1	2	3	4	5	6	7	8	9	10	11	12	13	14	15	16	17	18	
PAR	POSITION		4	4	4	3	4	4	3	4	4	4	4	3	4	3	5	4	5	4	TOTAL
Scott Verplank	T91	Round 1	5	4	5	3	5	5	4	4	4	5	4	3	5	3	5	4	5	4	77
USA	T16	Round 2	3	4	4	3	4	4	2	4	4	3	5	3	4	2	4	5	5	4	67
£10,650	T35	Round 3	6	4	5	3	4	5	4	4	5	4	4	5	4	3	5	3	5	5	78
	T58	Round 4	5	5	4	4	5	5	3	3	3	4	4	3	5	4	7	4	4	4	76 **-298**
Colin Montgomerie	T27	Round 1	4	5	4	2	5	4	4	4	4	6	4	2	4	3	5	4	5	4	73
Scotland	T52	Round 2	4	6	4	3	7	6	2	3	4	4	4	3	4	3	5	5	4	4	75
£10,650	T35	Round 3	4	5	4	3	4	5	4	4	4	5	4	3	4	3	5	3	5	5	74
	T58	Round 4	5	4	4	4	4	5	3	5	4	4	3	3	5	4	5	4	5	5	76 **-298**
Peter Hanson	T7	Round 1	4	3	4	3	4	5	3	3	4	5	5	4	4	2	5	4	5	4	71
Sweden	T11	Round 2	3	4	4	4	4	5	4	3	5	3	4	3	4	3	6	5	4	4	72
£10,650	T27	Round 3	4	4	4	4	5	5	3	4	4	7	5	4	4	3	5	4	4	5	78
	T58	Round 4	4	4	4	3	4	5	3	4	4	6	8	4	4	3	4	4	5	4	77 **-298**
Wen Chong Liang	T91	Round 1	5	4	4	4	5	4	3	4	4	4	4	3	5	3	6	4	6	5	77
China	T52	Round 2	6	4	4	3	3	5	2	4	4	4	4	4	4	3	5	4	4	4	71
£10,200	T64	Round 3	4	5	5	6	4	5	3	4	4	5	4	3	4	3	5	4	5	4	77
	T64	Round 4	5	4	4	3	4	4	3	4	3	4	4	3	4	4	5	4	7	5	74 **-299**
Jonathan Lomas	T52	Round 1	4	5	4	4	5	4	3	4	4	3	5	3	4	4	4	5	6	4	75
England	T52	Round 2	4	6	4	4	5	4	3	4	4	4	4	2	4	3	6	4	4	4	73
£10,200	T59	Round 3	5	4	4	3	6	4	3	3	4	5	5	3	5	4	5	4	5	4	76
	T64	Round 4	4	4	4	4	5	4	4	4	4	5	3	3	4	3	5	4	6	5	75 **-299**
Soren Hansen	T52	Round 1	4	5	4	3	4	5	3	4	4	4	4	4	5	3	4	4	7	4	75
Denmark	T16	Round 2	4	4	4	3	4	4	2	4	4	4	4	3	4	3	5	5	4	4	69
£10,200	T27	Round 3	4	4	5	4	4	6	4	4	4	5	4	3	4	4	5	4	5	4	77
	T64	Round 4	6	4	4	4	4	5	3	4	5	5	4	3	4	3	5	4	5	6	78 **-299**
Lee Westwood	T52	Round 1	5	6	5	3	4	5	3	4	5	3	4	3	4	3	5	4	5	4	75
England	T69	Round 2	5	4	4	3	4	5	3	4	4	5	4	3	4	4	5	4	5	4	74
£9,900	T76	Round 3	6	5	4	3	5	5	3	4	4	6	4	3	4	4	6	4	4	4	78
	T67	Round 4	4	4	5	4	3	5	3	4	4	6	4	3	4	3	5	4	4	4	73 **-300**
David Horsey	T38	Round 1	5	4	4	4	3	6	3	4	4	4	5	3	4	3	5	5	4	4	74
England	T16	Round 2	4	4	4	3	4	5	4	4	3	5	5	3	4	4	5	3	3	3	70
£9,900	T48	Round 3	5	5	5	4	5	6	4	5	4	4	4	3	4	3	5	4	4	5	79
	T67	Round 4	6	4	5	3	5	5	3	5	4	4	5	3	5	3	5	3	5	4	77 **-300**
Jean-Baptiste Gonnet	T52	Round 1	4	4	4	3	5	5	3	3	5	4	4	3	5	3	6	4	6	4	75
France	T38	Round 2	4	5	4	3	3	4	3	5	4	5	4	3	3	3	5	4	6	4	72
£9,900	T20	Round 3	4	4	4	4	3	5	3	3	4	4	4	4	4	3	5	5	5	5	73
	T67	Round 4	5	4	5	4	4	7	3	3	5	4	4	3	5	3	5	4	6	6	80 **-300**
Brendan Jones	T38	Round 1	5	5	4	3	3	5	3	4	5	4	4	4	4	3	5	3	5	5	74
Australia	T38	Round 2	4	4	4	3	4	5	3	4	4	4	5	3	4	5	5	4	4	4	73
£9,350	T82	Round 3	5	4	5	4	4	5	4	5	4	5	4	7	4	3	5	6	4	5	83
	T70	Round 4	5	4	4	3	3	3	4	4	4	4	4	3	4	3	4	5	6	4	71 **-301**
Justin Rose	T38	Round 1	4	5	4	3	4	6	3	4	5	4	4	3	4	3	5	4	5	4	74
England	T27	Round 2	4	5	4	2	3	5	3	4	4	5	4	2	5	3	5	5	5	4	72
£9,350	T79	Round 3	5	4	5	4	6	5	4	5	4	5	4	3	5	3	5	4	6	5	82
	T70	Round 4	4	5	3	4	3	5	3	4	4	4	5	4	5	3	4	4	5	4	73 **-301**
Martin Wiegele	T52	Round 1	4	4	5	2	5	4	3	4	4	4	4	3	4	3	5	7	6	4	75
Austria	T69	Round 2	4	3	5	3	4	5	3	5	4	4	4	3	5	3	4	5	6	4	74
£9,350	T76	Round 3	4	5	4	3	5	5	3	4	4	3	4	3	7	5	5	5	5	4	78
	T70	Round 4	5	4	5	4	4	4	3	4	5	5	4	3	5	3	5	3	4	4	74 **-301**
John Rollins	T27	Round 1	5	5	4	3	4	5	3	4	4	4	5	3	4	3	5	5	4	3	73
USA	T52	Round 2	4	5	3	3	4	4	4	4	5	4	5	3	4	3	6	5	5	4	75
£9,350	T64	Round 3	7	4	4	3	5	5	4	3	4	6	4	2	5	4	5	4	4	4	77
	T70	Round 4	4	4	5	4	5	6	3	4	5	4	4	3	4	3	5	4	4	5	76 **-301**

HOLE			1	2	3	4	5	6	7	8	9	10	11	12	13	14	15	16	17	18	
PAR	POSITION		4	4	4	3	4	4	3	4	4	4	4	3	4	3	5	4	5	4	TOTAL
Craig Parry	T91	Round 1	4	5	4	3	5	5	3	4	4	5	5	2	4	4	6	4	5	5	77
Australia	T38	Round 2	4	3	3	3	4	4	3	5	4	4	5	3	4	3	5	4	5	4	70
£9,350	T59	Round 3	4	5	4	4	4	4	4	4	4	5	4	3	6	3	6	4	5	4	77
	T70	Round 4	6	4	4	3	4	5	3	4	5	4	4	3	5	3	6	5	5	4	77 -301
Jose-Filipe Lima	T27	Round 1	5	5	4	3	3	5	2	5	4	4	4	3	4	4	5	5	4	4	73
Portugal	T69	Round 2	4	4	4	3	5	7	3	4	4	4	4	3	5	3	6	5	4	4	76
£9,350	T59	Round 3	4	4	4	4	4	5	3	4	5	4	5	3	4	4	4	5	4	5	75
	T70	Round 4	5	4	4	5	4	5	4	4	4	6	4	3	5	3	4	4	5	4	77 -301
Jeff Overton	T15	Round 1	5	3	4	3	4	5	4	3	4	4	5	5	4	3	4	4	4	4	72
USA	T38	Round 2	4	4	5	4	3	4	4	3	5	4	5	3	4	4	6	5	4	4	75
£9,350	T35	Round 3	4	4	4	3	4	6	2	4	4	4	4	4	5	3	6	4	5	5	75
	T70	Round 4	5	5	4	4	4	5	3	4	5	4	6	2	6	4	4	5	5	4	79 -301
Pablo Larrazabal	T52	Round 1	5	5	4	2	4	4	3	4	6	4	4	3	5	3	5	4	5	5	75
Spain	T69	Round 2	4	4	4	3	4	5	3	4	5	4	6	3	4	3	5	4	5	4	74
£9,350	T35	Round 3	4	6	3	3	4	5	3	3	5	4	4	3	6	2	5	4	5	4	73
	T70	Round 4	5	5	5	3	4	5	4	4	4	5	6	3	4	2	6	5	6	3	79 -301
Lucas Glover	T110	Round 1	5	5	4	2	3	5	4	4	5	4	4	4	5	4	6	5	5	4	78
USA	T69	Round 2	4	4	4	3	3	4	4	4	4	4	5	3	4	3	4	5	5	4	71
£8,850	T73	Round 3	7	5	4	3	5	4	4	4	4	4	4	5	3	4	5	3	4	5	77
	T78	Round 4	4	3	6	4	4	5	3	4	4	4	4	4	4	4	4	5	4	6	76 -302
Nick Dougherty	T52	Round 1	5	4	4	3	4	5	3	6	4	5	5	3	4	4	4	4	4	4	75
England	T27	Round 2	4	4	4	3	4	4	3	4	4	4	4	3	5	3	5	5	4	4	71
£8,850	T64	Round 3	5	5	4	4	6	5	5	5	4	4	4	3	5	3	5	4	5	3	79
	T78	Round 4	5	4	5	3	5	5	3	4	7	4	4	3	4	4	4	4	4	5	77 -302
Martin Kaymer	T52	Round 1	4	5	4	2	4	5	3	4	5	4	5	4	4	4	5	4	4	5	75
Germany	T38	Round 2	4	5	4	3	4	4	3	5	3	4	5	3	4	3	5	5	4	4	72
£8,700	T73	Round 3	5	4	5	3	4	5	3	4	5	5	5	4	4	4	6	4	4	5	79
	80	Round 4	4	4	4	3	4	6	4	5	7	4	4	3	4	3	5	5	4	4	77 -303
Phillip Archer	T52	Round 1	5	4	3	5	3	5	4	4	4	4	6	3	4	4	4	5	4	4	75
England	T69	Round 2	4	4	4	3	3	4	4	5	3	4	5	4	5	4	4	5	5	4	74
£8,600	T76	Round 3	4	4	5	3	4	4	4	5	5	4	5	3	5	3	6	6	5	4	78
	81	Round 4	3	4	4	4	4	5	3	5	4	5	4	4	4	4	5	5	5	5	77 -304
Sean O'Hair	T52	Round 1	4	4	5	3	5	5	3	4	4	4	4	3	4	4	5	5	5	4	75
USA	T52	Round 2	4	5	4	3	4	5	3	4	4	4	5	3	5	3	5	4	4	4	73
£8,500	T79	Round 3	4	4	4	4	5	4	4	4	4	4	3	4	4	3	5	4	9	7	80
	82	Round 4	4	5	5	3	4	4	4	4	4	3	4	3	6	3	6	4	7	5	78 -306
Chih-Bing Lam	T15	Round 1	5	3	4	3	4	5	3	4	4	5	5	2	5	3	4	5	4	4	72
Singapore	T38	Round 2	7	4	5	2	4	5	3	4	5	3	5	3	5	4	4	4	4	4	75
£8,400	T82	Round 3	5	4	3	3	5	5	4	4	6	6	4	4	6	4	5	4	7	4	83
	83	Round 4	5	7	5	3	4	6	3	4	5	5	4	2	5	3	7	4	5	4	81 -311

NON QUALIFIERS AFTER 36 HOLES

(Leading 10 professionals and ties receive £3,200 each, next 20 professionals and ties receive £2,650 each, next 20 professionals and ties receive £2,375 each, remainder of professionals receive £2,100 each.)

HOLE			1	2	3	4	5	6	7	8	9	10	11	12	13	14	15	16	17	18	
PAR	POSITION		4	4	4	3	4	4	3	4	4	4	4	3	4	3	5	4	5	4	TOTAL
Paul Lawrie	T91	Round 1	5	4	5	2	5	5	3	4	4	4	5	3	4	3	5	4	7	5	77
Scotland	**T84**	Round 2	4	4	3	3	5	4	3	4	4	4	4	3	4	4	6	5	5	4	73-**150**
Stewart Cink	T52	Round 1	4	5	4	3	4	4	4	5	3	4	5	4	4	4	6	4	4	4	75
USA	**T84**	Round 2	4	4	4	4	4	4	3	4	4	5	5	4	4	3	5	5	5	4	75-**150**
Azuna Yano	T38	Round 1	5	4	4	4	5	3	4	4	3	5	5	3	4	3	4	5	5	4	74
Japan	**T84**	Round 2	4	4	4	4	4	4	4	4	5	4	4	3	5	3	6	4	5	5	76-**150**
James Kingston	T91	Round 1	5	4	5	3	5	3	4	5	4	6	4	3	4	5	5	4	4	4	77
South Africa	**T84**	Round 2	4	4	4	4	4	4	2	5	4	4	4	4	3	5	5	4	5	73-**150**
Prayad Marksaeng	T91	Round 1	5	4	4	2	6	5	3	4	4	5	6	3	4	3	5	4	6	4	77
Thailand	**T84**	Round 2	4	5	4	3	4	5	3	3	3	5	4	3	5	2	4	6	5	5	73-**150**
Scott McCarron	T52	Round 1	4	4	4	3	5	5	3	4	4	3	5	4	4	4	5	4	6	4	75
USA	**T84**	Round 2	3	4	4	3	3	5	5	4	4	3	7	4	4	4	5	5	4	4	75-**150**
Peter Baker	T52	Round 1	4	5	5	4	3	5	4	4	3	4	4	4	5	4	4	4	5	4	75
England	**T84**	Round 2	5	4	4	3	3	4	3	4	5	5	5	3	4	2	6	4	6	5	75-**150**
Alex Cejka	T74	Round 1	4	4	3	4	4	4	3	6	4	5	5	3	5	3	5	4	5	5	76
Germany	**T84**	Round 2	5	4	4	3	5	5	3	4	4	4	4	3	5	3	4	5	5	4	74-**150**
Yoshinobu Tsukada	T52	Round 1	6	5	4	2	5	5	3	4	4	4	4	3	4	3	4	5	6	4	75
Japan	**T84**	Round 2	5	4	4	4	4	4	4	5	4	4	4	3	5	3	5	5	4	4	75-**150**
Peter Appleyard	T38	Round 1	4	4	3	3	4	6	3	5	4	5	5	3	4	3	5	5	4	4	74
England	**T84**	Round 2	4	4	4	3	4	6	4	4	4	5	6	3	4	3	5	4	4	5	76-**150**
Pat Perez	T145	Round 1	5	4	5	2	5	5	3	4	4	4	5	4	5	4	5	7	7	4	82
USA	**T84**	Round 2	3	5	4	2	4	4	2	4	4	4	4	3	4	3	5	5	5	3	68-**150**
Damien McGrane	T123	Round 1	5	4	4	4	5	5	3	4	5	5	5	3	4	3	5	6	4	5	79
Republic of Ireland	**T84**	Round 2	4	4	4	3	4	4	3	4	4	4	5	3	5	3	5	5	4	3	71-**150**
Tom Watson	T38	Round 1	3	5	4	3	4	5	4	3	5	4	5	3	5	3	5	5	4	4	74
USA	**T84**	Round 2	4	4	4	3	4	4	4	5	4	4	5	3	5	4	6	5	4	4	76-**150**
Aaron Baddeley	T52	Round 1	4	4	4	4	4	4	3	4	5	5	5	4	5	3	4	5	4	4	75
Australia	**T84**	Round 2	5	4	4	4	5	5	3	4	4	5	5	3	3	3	4	5	5	4	75-**150**
Richard Sterne	T110	Round 1	5	4	4	4	4	5	3	6	5	4	6	3	4	3	5	5	4	4	78
South Africa	**T84**	Round 2	4	4	4	3	4	5	3	4	5	5	4	3	4	3	5	5	4	4	72-**150**
Pelle Edberg	T74	Round 1	6	4	5	4	5	3	3	4	4	4	4	3	4	2	5	5	6	5	76
Sweden	**T84**	Round 2	5	4	4	3	3	5	4	4	4	4	4	5	4	3	5	5	4	4	74-**150**
Jon Bevan	T110	Round 1	5	6	4	4	3	5	5	4	4	4	6	3	4	3	5	5	4	4	78
England	**T84**	Round 2	4	4	5	3	4	3	4	3	4	5	5	4	3	3	2	5	5	5	4	72-**150**
Joshua Cunliffe	T123	Round 1	4	5	4	4	4	5	3	5	4	5	4	5	4	4	5	4	7	3	79
South Africa	**T84**	Round 2	5	5	4	3	4	5	3	4	4	4	3	3	4	3	5	4	4	4	71-**150**
Andrew Tampion	T110	Round 1	6	5	4	3	4	5	3	4	4	5	4	4	5	3	6	4	5	4	78
Australia	**T102**	Round 2	5	4	4	3	4	5	3	5	4	3	4	4	5	4	4	4	4	4	73-**151**
Mark O'Meara	T38	Round 1	5	4	4	4	4	5	4	4	4	5	4	3	4	3	5	4	4	4	74
USA	**T102**	Round 2	5	5	3	3	3	5	3	4	4	5	5	4	5	3	5	5	7	3	77-**151**
Charles Howell III	T74	Round 1	5	4	4	4	4	5	3	4	4	5	5	4	4	4	5	4	4	4	76
USA	**T102**	Round 2	6	4	4	4	4	4	4	4	5	4	5	3	4	3	5	4	4	4	75-**151**
Ryuji Imada	T91	Round 1	6	3	4	3	5	5	2	5	3	4	5	4	3	3	6	5	6	5	77
Japan	**T102**	Round 2	5	4	4	3	3	5	4	6	5	3	4	4	4	4	4	4	4	4	74-**151**

HOLE			1	2	3	4	5	6	7	8	9	10	11	12	13	14	15	16	17	18	
PAR	POSITION		4	4	4	3	4	4	3	4	4	4	4	3	4	3	5	4	5	4	TOTAL
Brandt Snedeker	T15	Round 1	5	4	5	4	5	5	2	5	4	3	4	3	4	3	5	4	4	3	72
USA	T102	Round 2	4	5	3	4	6	5	2	3	5	5	4	4	5	4	5	5	5	5	79 -151
Soren Kjeldsen	T143	Round 1	5	5	4	4	4	5	3	4	6	4	6	3	5	4	6	4	4	5	81
Denmark	T102	Round 2	3	5	4	3	4	5	3	4	3	4	5	2	5	3	4	4	4	5	70 -151
Mark Calcavecchia	T74	Round 1	4	6	4	3	4	5	3	5	4	5	4	3	4	3	5	6	4	4	76
USA	T102	Round 2	5	4	3	3	5	4	3	4	5	4	4	3	5	4	5	4	5	5	75 -151
Geoff Ogilvy	T91	Round 1	4	5	5	3	4	5	3	5	3	4	4	3	5	4	5	5	5	4	77
Australia	T102	Round 2	3	4	4	3	4	4	3	5	4	4	6	3	5	3	4	6	5	4	74 -151
Oliver Wilson	T91	Round 1	4	4	5	2	4	6	4	5	5	4	5	3	5	3	5	4	5	4	77
England	T102	Round 2	5	4	4	3	4	5	3	4	4	5	4	3	5	3	5	4	5	4	74 -151
Vijay Singh	T136	Round 1	6	5	4	3	5	5	4	5	5	5	5	3	5	3	5	4	4	4	80
Fiji	T102	Round 2	3	4	3	4	5	5	4	4	4	3	5	3	4	3	4	4	5	4	71 -151
Hideto Tanihara	T74	Round 1	6	5	4	3	4	6	4	4	4	5	3	3	4	3	6	4	4	4	76
Japan	T102	Round 2	5	4	4	4	4	4	3	4	5	4	4	3	4	3	6	5	5	4	75 -151
Craig Barlow	T123	Round 1	5	5	4	3	5	4	2	4	4	4	4	3	6	3	7	5	6	5	79
USA	T102	Round 2	4	4	4	3	4	4	3	4	4	4	5	3	4	3	5	6	4	4	72 -151
David Smail	T74	Round 1	5	5	5	3	4	5	3	4	4	5	5	3	5	3	5	4	4	4	76
New Zealand	T114	Round 2	5	4	3	3	5	4	3	4	5	5	6	3	4	3	5	5	5	4	76 -152
Michael Letzig	T110	Round 1	4	5	5	3	4	5	3	4	4	7	6	2	4	4	6	5	4	3	78
USA	T114	Round 2	4	4	3	3	4	5	3	3	4	4	5	7	5	4	4	5	4	3	74 -152
Niclas Fasth	T123	Round 1	5	4	4	3	3	5	3	5	4	5	6	3	5	3	6	4	6	5	79
Sweden	T114	Round 2	4	4	4	3	4	5	3	4	4	3	5	4	4	3	7	4	4	4	73 -152
Benjamin Hebert*	T123	Round 1	5	5	4	3	4	5	5	4	4	5	5	3	4	4	5	5	5	4	79
France	T114	Round 2	4	3	4	2	4	4	4	4	4	4	4	4	5	3	5	5	5	5	73 -152
Johan Edfors	T110	Round 1	5	5	5	3	3	5	3	4	4	4	6	3	4	4	5	5	5	4	78
Sweden	T114	Round 2	4	4	4	2	4	4	3	4	4	4	6	3	4	5	4	5	5	4	74 -152
Simon Dyson	T145	Round 1	4	5	4	3	5	5	3	4	6	9	5	3	3	3	5	5	5	4	82
England	T114	Round 2	4	5	4	3	4	5	3	4	4	4	4	3	4	3	5	4	4	3	70 -152
Matt Kuchar	T123	Round 1	4	5	3	3	5	4	4	4	5	5	5	3	4	3	5	5	4	4	79
USA	T114	Round 2	5	4	4	3	3	6	3	4	4	4	4	3	4	3	5	5	5	4	73 -152
Hunter Mahan	T136	Round 1	4	4	4	4	4	6	5	4	5	5	5	4	5	2	7	4	4	4	80
USA	T114	Round 2	4	4	4	3	4	4	2	4	5	4	4	3	4	3	5	5	6	4	72 -152
Paul Goydos	T91	Round 1	4	5	4	4	5	6	4	4	5	4	4	3	4	3	5	5	4	4	77
USA	T114	Round 2	4	4	4	3	4	6	3	4	4	4	5	3	5	4	6	4	4	4	75 -152
Barry Hume	T74	Round 1	5	4	5	3	5	5	3	4	5	5	4	3	5	4	5	3	5	3	76
Scotland	T114	Round 2	5	4	4	3	4	6	3	4	4	4	5	3	5	3	7	3	5	4	76 -152
Tim Clark	T74	Round 1	4	5	4	3	4	5	3	4	4	8	4	3	5	2	6	4	4	3	76
South Africa	T124	Round 2	5	5	4	4	4	5	4	4	5	3	5	3	4	4	5	5	4	4	77 -153
Boo Weekley	T136	Round 1	5	5	4	4	4	4	4	5	4	5	5	3	5	3	6	4	6	4	80
USA	T124	Round 2	4	4	4	3	4	5	3	4	4	6	3	3	4	3	4	5	6	4	73 -153
Gary Boyd	T91	Round 1	5	5	4	2	4	4	3	5	4	5	5	4	4	3	6	4	5	5	77
England	T124	Round 2	4	3	4	3	4	5	6	4	3	4	4	3	5	3	6	6	5	4	76 -153
Angel Cabrera	T91	Round 1	4	4	4	3	3	5	4	6	3	4	5	4	4	4	6	4	5	5	77
Argentina	T127	Round 2	4	4	4	3	4	5	3	4	4	5	5	3	5	3	6	3	6	6	77 -154
Rory Sabbatini	T123	Round 1	5	4	4	3	4	6	3	4	7	5	4	3	4	3	5	5	7	3	79
South Africa	T127	Round 2	5	4	4	4	4	8	3	4	4	4	5	3	3	4	4	4	4	4	75 -154
Miguel A Jimenez	T15	Round 1	4	5	4	3	4	5	4	4	4	4	4	3	3	4	4	4	5	4	72
Spain	T127	Round 2	5	5	4	4	6	5	3	6	4	4	5	4	5	4	5	5	4	4	82 -154

HOLE			1	2	3	4	5	6	7	8	9	10	11	12	13	14	15	16	17	18	
PAR	POSITION		4	4	4	3	4	4	3	4	4	4	4	3	4	3	5	4	5	4	TOTAL
Rod Pampling	T91	Round 1	5	7	4	4	3	4	3	4	4	4	5	3	4	3	7	4	5	4	77
Australia	**T127**	Round 2	4	5	4	4	4	5	4	5	3	4	5	3	4	3	5	5	6	4	77 -**154**
Angelo Que	T74	Round 1	5	4	4	4	5	5	4	4	4	4	4	3	5	4	4	6	4	3	76
Philippines	**T127**	Round 2	4	4	4	3	3	5	4	6	5	5	4	3	4	4	5	6	4	5	78 -**154**
Douglas McGuigan	T123	Round 1	3	5	4	4	4	5	3	5	5	5	5	4	4	4	5	4	6	4	79
Scotland	**T127**	Round 2	4	4	4	3	4	5	3	4	4	4	4	3	5	3	6	5	6	4	75 -**154**
Jeff Quinney	T123	Round 1	5	5	6	3	4	6	3	4	4	5	5	3	3	3	7	5	4	4	79
USA	**T127**	Round 2	4	5	3	3	5	4	3	4	3	5	5	3	5	3	5	5	5	5	75 -**154**
Ewan Porter	T74	Round 1	4	4	4	3	5	4	3	6	4	5	5	3	4	4	5	4	5	4	76
Australia	**T134**	Round 2	4	4	4	3	7	5	3	4	4	5	7	2	5	3	7	3	5	4	79 -**155**
Rohan Blizard*	T110	Round 1	4	6	5	2	4	5	3	5	4	4	4	4	4	3	7	4	5	5	78
Australia	**T134**	Round 2	4	4	4	4	4	4	3	4	4	5	4	3	4	4	6	4	6	6	77 -**155**
Hennie Otto	T123	Round 1	5	4	5	3	4	5	3	4	5	4	5	4	5	3	5	5	5	5	79
South Africa	**T136**	Round 2	4	4	4	2	3	4	4	5	5	7	4	4	4	3	7	4	5	4	77 -**156**
Scott Strange	152	Round 1	4	6	6	4	4	6	3	4	4	5	4	4	5	3	5	5	6	6	84
Australia	**T136**	Round 2	4	5	4	3	4	5	3	5	3	5	5	3	4	3	4	4	4	4	72 -**156**
J B Holmes	T123	Round 1	6	5	4	3	3	5	3	4	6	6	4	4	4	3	5	5	4	5	79
USA	**T136**	Round 2	5	8	4	4	3	5	3	4	3	4	4	4	4	3	5	5	5	4	77 -**156**
Jamie Elson	T110	Round 1	5	5	5	4	4	5	3	4	5	4	4	3	4	3	5	4	6	5	78
England	**T136**	Round 2	5	4	4	3	5	5	4	4	6	5	5	3	4	3	5	4	5	4	78 -**156**
Hiroshi Iwata	T27	Round 1	4	4	5	3	5	5	2	4	3	4	4	3	4	3	5	5	6	4	73
Japan	**T140**	Round 2	5	5	5	3	3	6	3	4	8	4	5	3	5	4	5	7	5	4	84 -**157**
Reinier Saxton*	T136	Round 1	5	5	4	4	4	5	3	5	5	5	4	4	5	3	6	4	5	4	80
Netherlands	**T140**	Round 2	5	5	5	4	4	4	3	4	4	6	4	5	4	3	5	4	4	4	77 -**157**
Michio Matsumura	T145	Round 1	4	6	5	4	6	5	3	5	5	4	5	3	5	4	5	4	5	4	82
Japan	**T142**	Round 2	4	4	4	3	4	5	4	4	5	4	6	3	5	3	5	4	5	4	76 -**158**
Tim Petrovic	T145	Round 1	5	4	5	3	4	7	4	4	4	7	5	3	5	4	5	5	4	4	82
USA	**T142**	Round 2	6	5	3	4	4	5	3	3	5	3	3	3	6	4	5	4	6	4	76 -**158**
Adam Blyth	T143	Round 1	4	5	5	3	4	6	4	6	4	5	6	3	3	4	5	5	5	4	81
Australia	**T142**	Round 2	4	4	4	3	4	6	3	4	4	5	5	4	5	4	5	5	4	4	77 -**158**
Steve Webster	T123	Round 1	4	6	5	3	5	4	2	4	6	5	6	4	4	4	4	5	4	4	79
England	**T145**	Round 2	6	4	4	4	3	5	3	5	5	5	5	3	4	3	6	7	4	4	80 -**159**
Philip Walton	T91	Round 1	6	5	4	3	4	6	3	4	3	5	4	3	5	3	5	4	5	5	77
Republic of Ireland	**T145**	Round 2	5	6	4	4	4	5	3	4	5	5	4	4	5	4	7	4	5	4	82 -**159**
Bradley Lamb	T153	Round 1	5	6	5	4	5	5	3	5	4	6	5	4	4	4	5	5	5	5	85
Australia	**T145**	Round 2	4	4	5	3	5	5	4	3	4	4	4	2	4	4	5	4	5	5	74 -**159**
Darren Fichardt	T145	Round 1	6	5	5	4	5	4	4	4	4	6	5	4	4	3	4	4	6	5	82
South Africa	**T148**	Round 2	4	4	4	2	4	5	3	5	6	4	6	3	5	4	5	4	4	6	78 -**160**
Jerry Kelly	151	Round 1	5	4	4	4	5	6	4	4	5	5	5	3	3	4	6	7	5	4	83
USA	**T148**	Round 2	5	5	3	3	4	4	5	4	4	4	4	4	4	3	5	5	6	5	77 -**160**
Shintaro Kai	T136	Round 1	3	4	4	4	5	6	3	4	4	4	5	5	4	3	6	5	6	5	80
Japan	**150**	Round 2	4	6	3	4	5	3	3	4	5	4	5	4	6	4	5	5	6	5	81 -**161**
Danny Chia	T74	Round 1	4	5	4	3	4	4	3	5	4	5	4	5	5	3	5	5	4	4	76
Malaysia	**151**	Round 2	6	4	4	4	4	5	3	5	6	6	5	5	6	3	7	6	5	5	87 -**163**
Peter Fowler	T145	Round 1	6	5	4	3	4	6	4	5	4	5	6	2	4	3	6	5	6	4	82
Australia	**152**	Round 2	6	5	4	3	4	4	4	5	5	4	6	3	4	3	10	4	5	3	82 -**164**
John Daly	T136	Round 1	5	5	4	3	4	4	3	5	4	5	5	3	6	3	7	5	5	4	80
USA	**T153**	Round 2	4	5	4	3	4	6	4	5	5	5	6	3	9	4	6	6	5	5	89 -**169**

HOLE			1	2	3	4	5	6	7	8	9	10	11	12	13	14	15	16	17	18	
PAR	POSITION		4	4	4	3	4	4	3	4	4	4	4	3	4	3	5	4	5	4	TOTAL
Jamie Howarth	T153	Round 1	6	5	6	3	6	6	3	7	4	4	5	2	4	3	6	6	5	4	85
England	**T153**	Round 2	5	4	3	3	4	5	4	4	6	5	5	3	5	4	7	6	5	6	84 -**169**
Sandy Lyle	T155	Round 1	5	4	4	4	5	5	5	6	7	4									**WD**
Scotland																					
Rich Beem	T155	Round 1	5	8	5	4	5	5	5	4	5										**WD**
USA																					

THE TOP TENS Courtesy of Unisys

Eagles/Birdies
1. Anders Hansen 0/14
2. Padraig Harrington 2/11
3. Stephen Ames 0/11
3. Adam Scott 0/11
3. Camilo Villegas 0/11
3. Thomas Aiken 0/11
3. David Duval 0/11
3. Retief Goosen 0/11
9. 6 players tied 0/10

Pars
1. Davis Love III 55
2. Gregory Bourdy 52
3. Graeme McDowell 51
3. Soren Hansen 51
5. Jim Furyk 50
5. Steve Stricker 50
5. Anthony Kim 50
5. Woody Austin 50
9. 4 players tied 49
58. Padraig Harrington 42

Bogeys
1. Phillip Archer 26
2. Martin Kaymer 24
3. Tom Gillis 23
3. David Horsey 23
3. Justin Rose 23
3. Jeff Overton 23
3. Lucas Glover 23
3. Chih-Bing Lam 23
9. 3 players tied 22
55. Padraig Harrington 16

Double Bogeys/Worse
1. Jamie Howarth 9/1
2. Chih-Bing Lam 6/2
3. Danny Chia 7/0
4. Peter Fowler 5/1
4. John Daly 5/1
6. Darren Fichardt 5/0
6. Jean Van de Velde 5/0
6. Pablo Larrazbal 5/0
9. 3 players tied 4/1
118. Padraig Harrington 1/0

Driving Distance
1. Paul Waring 311.9
2. Adam Scott 309.8
3. Soren Hansen 307.5
4. David Duval 307.4
5. Robert Allenby 307.3
6. Andres Romero 306.1
7. Davis Love III 305.8
8. Paul Casey 304.8
9. Alexander Noren 303.6
10. David Howell 303.4
45. Padraig Harrington 292.1

Fairways Hit
Maximum of 56
1. Jonathan Lomas 39
1. Bart Bryant 39
3. Anders Hansen 37
4. Peter Hanson 36
4. Gregory Havret 36
4. Henrik Stenson 36
7. Ross Fisher 35
7. Michael Campbell 35
7. Simon Khan 35
10. 6 players tied 34
35. Padraig Harrington 29

Greens in Regulation
Maximum of 72
1. Anthony Kim 50
2. Paul Casey 49
3. Robert Allenby 45
3. Robert Karlsson 45
5. Jim Furyk 44
5. Phil Mickelson 44
7. Ian Poulter 43
7. David Howell 43
7. Davis Love III 43
10. 5 players tied 42
30. Padraig Harrington 38

Putts
1. David Frost 107
2. Gregory Bourdy 108
3. Andres Romero 111
4. Graeme Storm 113
5. Greg Norman 114
6. Lucas Glover 115
7. Stephen Ames 116
7. Padraig Harrington 116
7. Richard Green 116
10. 7 players tied 117

EAGLES — Others with one each: David Howell, Paul Casey, Robert Allenby, Anthony Kim, Ben Curtis, Jean Van de Velde, Gregory Havret, Thomas Sherreard, Mike Weir, David Horsey

Statistical Rankings

Courtesy of Unisys

	Driving Distance	Rank	Fairways Hit	Rank	Greens In Regulation	Rank	Putts	Rank		Driving Distance	Rank	Fairways Hit	Rank	Greens In Regulation	Rank	Putts	Rank
Thomas Aiken	296.0	27	21	76	35	57	118	17	Zach Johnson	278.8	76	34	10	36	49	117	10
Robert Allenby	307.3	5	31	26	45	3	132	81	Brendan Jones	299.5	20	20	81	30	75	119	22
Stephen Ames	288.0	55	27	51	37	37	116	7	Robert Karlsson	294.3	35	27	51	45	3	125	64
Stuart Appleby	292.6	41	25	62	33	69	120	29	Martin Kaymer	303.3	11	17	83	32	72	123	49
Phillip Archer	291.3	48	29	35	29	77	120	29	Simon Khan	291.8	47	35	7	38	30	122	42
Woody Austin	281.3	71	31	26	42	10	125	64	Anthony Kim	301.4	14	30	32	50	1	132	81
Gregory Bourdy	294.3	35	29	35	29	77	108	2	Doug Labelle II	267.3	82	29	35	42	10	127	75
Bart Bryant	283.6	64	39	1	42	10	127	75	Chih-Bing Lam	296.8	25	28	46	37	37	130	80
Michael Campbell	292.1	45	35	7	41	15	125	64	Pablo Larrazabal	295.4	29	28	46	39	21	124	59
Ariel Canete	295.5	28	24	68	36	49	123	49	Tom Lehman	281.1	72	33	16	38	30	120	29
Paul Casey	304.8	8	33	16	49	2	132	81	Justin Leonard	294.6	33	27	51	35	57	118	17
KJ Choi	295.0	31	31	26	42	10	123	39	Wen Chong Liang	283.5	65	28	46	37	37	121	36
Ben Curtis	299.5	20	27	51	36	49	119	22	Jose-Filipe Lima	286.4	59	29	35	34	65	120	29
Nick Dougherty	302.4	12	26	56	34	65	124	59	Jonathan Lomas	276.1	78	39	1	37	37	127	75
David Duval	307.4	4	25	62	36	49	121	36	Davis Love III	305.8	7	23	72	43	7	126	72
Ernie Els	300.1	17	31	26	35	57	117	10	Graeme McDowell	292.9	39	25	62	41	15	124	59
Richard Finch	282.9	67	19	82	40	18	125	64	Rocco Mediate	274.0	79	32	21	37	37	118	17
Ross Fisher	300.6	16	35	7	39	21	125	64	Phil Mickelson	295.1	30	28	46	44	5	127	75
David Frost	289.1	53	21	76	24	83	107	1	Colin Montgomerie	282.6	68	29	35	35	57	118	17
Jim Furyk	295.0	31	31	26	44	5	123	49	Alexander Noren	303.6	9	26	56	39	21	124	59
Sergio Garcia	297.6	23	29	35	36	49	122	42	Greg Norman	293.8	37	21	76	37	37	114	5
Tom Gillis	287.0	56	34	10	33	69	120	29	Sean O'Hair	289.5	51	21	76	34	65	125	64
Lucas Glover	302.3	13	26	56	29	77	115	6	Nick O'Hern	267.9	81	33	16	39	21	125	64
Jean-Baptiste Gonnet	288.3	54	22	74	29	77	117	10	Jeff Overton	296.3	26	26	56	35	57	122	42
Retief Goosen	292.6	41	29	35	38	30	123	49	Craig Parry	261.5	83	32	21	28	82	118	17
Richard Green	271.8	80	24	68	32	72	116	7	Ian Poulter	290.3	50	34	10	43	7	121	36
Todd Hamilton	286.6	57	29	35	38	30	123	49	John Rollins	286.5	58	28	46	33	69	122	42
Anders Hansen	281.0	73	37	3	40	18	122	42	Andres Romero	306.1	6	32	21	30	75	111	3
Soren Hansen	307.5	3	29	35	36	49	125	64	Justin Rose	291.0	49	22	74	35	57	124	59
Peter Hanson	281.5	69	36	4	35	57	121	36	Adam Scott	309.8	2	26	56	37	37	121	36
Padraig Harrington	292.1	45	29	35	38	30	116	7	Thomas Sherreard*	280.4	74	23	72	37	37	121	36
Gregory Havret	292.8	40	36	4	42	10	123	49	Heath Slocum	292.4	43	33	16	34	65	117	10
David Horsey	285.0	61	24	68	39	21	127	75	Kevin Stadler	294.4	34	21	76	32	72	117	10
David Howell	303.4	10	32	21	43	7	126	72	Henrik Stenson	300.0	18	36	4	37	37	119	22
Trevor Immelman	299.4	22	33	16	37	37	117	10	Graeme Storm	289.3	52	25	62	29	77	113	4
Fredrik Jacobson	277.3	77	25	62	39	21	122	42	Steve Stricker	283.5	65	27	51	39	21	120	29

	Driving Distance	Rank	Fairways Hit	Rank	Greens In Regulation	Rank	Putts	Rank
Jean Van de Velde	284.4	62	24	68	41	15	122	42
Scott Verplank	281.5	69	31	26	39	21	123	49
Camilo Villegas	297.0	24	25	62	36	49	120	29
Simon Wakefield	285.9	60	32	21	36	49	119	22
Anthony Wall	292.4	43	34	10	37	37	123	49
Paul Waring	311.9	1	34	10	40	18	119	22
Mike Weir	283.8	63	29	35	39	21	119	22
Lee Westwood	299.9	19	30	32	38	30	126	72
Martin Wiegele	293.5	38	34	10	35	57	123	49
Jay Williamson	279.3	75	26	56	38	30	119	22
Chris Wood*	300.9	15	30	32	37	37	117	10

Rank indicates position (including ties) after 72 holes.

NON QUALIFIERS AFTER 36 HOLES

	Driving Distance	Rank	Fairways Hit	Rank	Greens In Regulation	Rank	Putts	Rank
Peter Appleyard	306.5	4	13	106	19	39	58	36
Aaron Baddeley	286.0	68	12	124	12	138	57	25
Peter Baker	270.0	129	17	33	14	119	58	36
Craig Barlow	290.5	42	11	133	15	106	58	36
Jon Bevan	260.5	148	18	27	17	72	60	63
Rohan Blizard*	273.8	114	14	88	15	106	61	86
Adam Blyth	286.3	63	11	133	15	106	62	104
Gary Boyd	288.5	55	18	27	17	72	61	86
Angel Cabrera	297.3	14	13	106	12	138	57	25
Mark Calcavecchia	255.0	151	15	73	16	92	59	49
Alex Cejka	285.3	71	18	27	18	55	60	63
Danny Chia	282.5	82	9	150	14	119	62	104
Stewart Cink	301.0	9	14	88	16	92	61	86
Tim Clark	280.0	96	19	15	16	92	63	117
Joshua Cunliffe	295.5	22	16	51	16	92	60	63
John Daly	289.0	52	8	153	12	138	68	153
Simon Dyson	273.8	114	17	33	19	39	61	86
Pelle Edberg	304.3	7	11	133	18	55	61	86
Johan Edfors	295.8	21	15	73	14	119	60	63
Jamie Elson	253.5	154	9	150	20	26	68	153
Niclas Fasth	268.0	135	14	88	15	106	63	117
Darren Fichardt	256.5	150	13	106	11	145	61	86
Peter Fowler	278.5	101	11	133	13	131	61	86
Paul Goydos	282.3	85	19	15	16	92	63	117
Benjamin Hebert*	274.3	113	16	51	18	55	64	132
J B Holmes	277.5	105	13	106	16	92	60	63
Jamie Howarth	265.3	142	11	133	13	131	62	104
Charles Howell III	291.0	40	12	124	19	39	64	132
Barry Hume	275.8	110	13	106	14	119	60	63
Ryuji Imada	272.5	125	17	33	14	119	55	10
Hiroshi Iwata	265.5	140	16	51	20	26	65	143
Miguel Angel Jimenez	277.0	108	21	3	14	119	64	132
Shintaro Kai	283.8	76	12	124	12	138	63	117
Jerry Kelly	254.5	152	13	106	15	106	64	132
James Kingston	289.0	52	17	33	14	119	60	63
Soren Kjeldsen	266.3	138	13	106	14	119	57	25
Matt Kuchar	265.3	142	13	106	15	106	61	86
Bradley Lamb	259.3	149	14	88	11	145	61	86
Paul Lawrie	279.5	98	16	51	10	151	54	6
Michael Letzig	289.3	51	13	106	19	39	63	117
Hunter Mahan	283.0	79	11	133	12	138	56	17
Prayad Marksaeng	290.3	43	14	88	17	72	57	25
Michio Matsumura	265.0	144	16	51	12	138	62	104
Scott McCarron	279.0	100	16	51	19	39	59	49
Damien McGrane	280.5	92	20	8	15	106	59	49
Douglas McGuigan	268.5	131	15	73	17	72	64	132
Geoff Ogilvy	286.5	62	10	145	7	154	52	3
Mark O'Meara	273.0	119	19	15	19	39	64	132
Hennie Otto	298.8	11	17	33	10	151	55	10
Rod Pampling	280.0	96	14	88	14	119	60	63
Pat Perez	282.0	88	12	124	16	92	57	25
Tim Petrovic	287.8	59	14	88	15	106	61	86
Ewan Porter	280.5	92	14	88	12	138	54	6
Angelo Que	286.3	63	11	133	14	119	59	49
Jeff Quinney	268.3	133	12	124	14	119	58	36
Rory Sabbatini	277.3	107	16	51	16	92	60	63
Reinier Saxton*	279.5	98	10	145	10	151	60	63
Vijay Singh	297.3	14	14	88	18	55	65	143
David Smail	287.3	60	17	33	15	106	60	63
Brandt Snedeker	269.3	130	16	51	15	106	63	117
Richard Sterne	292.0	35	14	88	17	72	61	86
Scott Strange	272.0	127	12	124	11	145	56	17
Andrew Tampion	280.8	91	18	27	18	55	63	117
Hideto Tanihara	276.0	109	15	73	13	131	56	17
Yoshinobu Tsukada	285.5	70	13	106	17	72	61	86
Philip Walton	273.0	119	16	51	13	131	63	117
Tom Watson	274.5	112	16	51	17	72	61	86
Steve Webster	290.0	45	10	145	16	92	67	150
Boo Weekley	296.3	18	16	51	17	72	62	104
Oliver Wilson	273.5	117	9	150	11	145	54	6
Azuma Yano	284.5	75	13	106	15	106	56	17

Rank indicates position (including ties) after 36 holes.

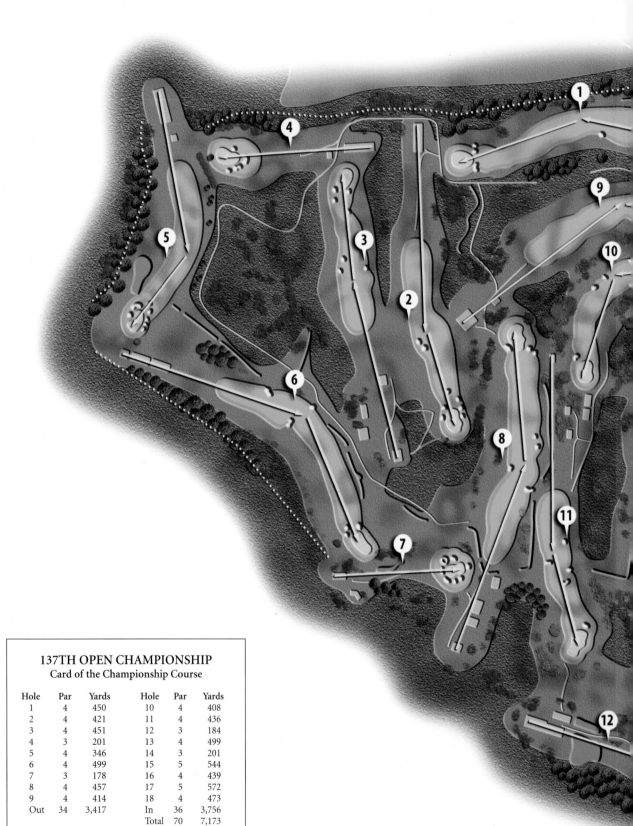

137TH OPEN CHAMPIONSHIP
Card of the Championship Course

Hole	Par	Yards	Hole	Par	Yards
1	4	450	10	4	408
2	4	421	11	4	436
3	4	451	12	3	184
4	3	201	13	4	499
5	4	346	14	3	201
6	4	499	15	5	544
7	3	178	16	4	439
8	4	457	17	5	572
9	4	414	18	4	473
Out	34	3,417	In	36	3,756
			Total	70	7,173